FROM CONDUCT TO CHARACTER:

A PRIMER IN ETHICAL THEORY

THIRD EDITION

Todd H. Speidell, Ph.D.

Wipf and Stock Publishers
EUGENE, OREGON

Wipf and Stock Publishers
199 West 8th Avenue, Suite 3
Eugene, Oregon 97401

From Conduct to Character:
A Primer in Ethical Theory
3rd Edition
By Todd H. Speidell
Copyright©2002 By Todd H. Speidell

ISBN: 1-57910-200-X

Find this and other titles online at: http://www.wipfandstock.com

To my students at

Webb School of Knoxville

CONTENTS

INTRODUCTION

Why write another book? "Of making many books there is no end," the author of Ecclesiastes wryly observes, "and much study wearies the body" (Eccl. 12:12). The immense record of published manuscripts confirms these ancient words, so why add to the tedium of life by writing another book?

Perhaps the best answer to the question is that another one is necessary. Even though ethics texts abound, a book that makes ethical theory accessible to budding ethicists would justify its existence. Books on ethical theory tend to be dry and pedantic, and even when they attempt to address real-life situations, they tend towards the abstract and hypothetical. Consider, for example, the classic lifeboat dilemma where the number of people exceeds the rations of food and water, leaving the moral inquirer in the quandary of deciding "What to do?" Presenting "pro" and "con" essays on various moral issues, ethics texts also tend to promote an inadvertent relativism: namely, that all moral issues are debatable (and those who disagree with this dogmatic assumption are labeled "dogmatic"!).

Valuing the integration of theory and practice and the use of real-life situations as a context for reflection, I have made ample use of the case study approach—that is, dilemmas that call for ethical reflection and resolution. My cases reflect the pain and anguish of real persons, although I have used fictional names to protect their identities when using confidential material. These cases do not pose abstract and hypothetical dilemmas even though it is sometimes true that "truth is stranger than fiction." (See the appendix of this third edition for cases and discussion of issues written by Webb Ethics students.)

This book focuses on several major western ethical traditions that usually guide, whether explicitly or implicitly, moral discussion and debate. Bringing these traditional assumptions to conscious awareness is one way of deepening ethical discourse by exposing the often unreflective assumptions with which we tend to operate. Examining these traditions and discussing key principles of moral reasoning should help elevate debates beyond the "Crossfire" approach (the shouting and yelling that passes for debate on CNN's nightly program) to civil and rational discourse. The point of studying ethics after all is not simply to enjoy good debate, but also, and even more importantly, to reflect on what it means to *be* and *become* virtuous people in our relationships with others.

I have written this short work specifically for my ethics students at Webb School of Knoxville, a private, independent, nonsectarian college prep school indebted to the Judeo-Christian tradition and committed to character formation. While this text might be suitable for college, seminary, or church settings—and I have used this material in these settings to lay a theoretical foundation for discussing moral issues, cases, and stories—I will use it with my own very capable high school students. I am indebted to their lively discussions, which make my job enjoyable and meaningful. I also appreciate the emphasis on honesty, respect, responsibility, leadership, and service that guides our school and creates a classroom context for candid discussion of issues of character.

I am also grateful to Jon Stock and Jim Tedrick of Wipf and Stock Publishers for their help in producing the third edition of this book, which now includes an extended Appendix that presents additional case studies and new "Framing the Issue" discussions of moral issues. The following people gave generously of their time to write constructive criticisms that improved the clarity of this work: Drs. Kevin Dodd and Chris Kettler. Residual errors or weaknesses, of course, remain my responsibility. Webb students Stephanie Helwig and Katherine Walker designed the cover of this book. Finally, my wife Dr. Gail Gnade's daily example of basing her life on conviction and integrity and our daughter Jessa Gnade Speidell's advancing concern to cultivate her nascent moral instincts provide for me models of virtuous living. They, along with friends, colleagues, and students at Webb School of Knoxville, have served as a community of character for me.

Todd Speidell
Todd_Speidell@webbschool.org

Part One:

Ethical Traditions

Duty is the necessity of acting from respect for the law.

> ➢ Immanuel Kant

THE CASE OF CORRIE TEN BOOM

In the film *The Hiding Place,* Corrie ten Boom and her family harbor Jews in their home to protect them from the Nazis. The ten Booms are a God-fearing Christian family, believing that loyalty to God must surpass loyalty to the state. As the Nazis knock on the ten Booms' door, the Jews go into their hiding place while Corrie stalls for time. When the Nazis finally break open the door, they first encounter Corrie and ask her, "Where are the Jews?"

➢ Is a lie justifiable under these circumstances?

➢ Do the ends justify the means?

10

➢ What should she do?

––

An ethic of duty, formally known as **deontology**, declares that one's actions are intrinsically right or wrong—irrespective of desirable ends, goals, or consequences. A deontologist affirms that one must do what is right, even if such moral behavior leads to negative consequences. The ends do not justify the means, deontologists believe, so people should not rationalize their actions by appealing to a "greater good"; instead, moral actions are based on duty and known through rules.

The philosopher Immanuel Kant (1724-1804) formulates an ethic of duty which insists that moral action must never be a means to an end but must be good in itself; an act must be done from duty and not with regard to consequences. His "categorical imperative" proscribes acts that do not have universal validity, insisting that one should only act on a maxim or principle of conduct that would hold true for everyone—e.g., "One ought to tell the truth as a matter of principle." He rejects by contrast a "hypothetical imperative," which is conditional or a means to another end—e.g., "If you want to avoid

punishment, you ought to tell the truth."
Furthermore, putting the same point more
personally, one ought to treat persons as ends in
themselves, never as a means to an end (Kant,
sections 8-10, 12-3 in Denise et al.).

> **Primary Source**: Immanuel Kant, *Fundamental
> Principles of the Metaphysics of Morals*
>
> "I am never to act otherwise than so *that I could
> also will that my maxim should become a universal
> law. . . .* Should I be content that my maxim
> (to extricate myself from difficulty by false
> promise) should hold good as a universal law,
> for myself as well as for others? And should I
> be able to say to myself, 'Everyone may make a
> deceitful promise when he finds himself in a
> difficulty from which he cannot otherwise
> extricate himself'? Then I presently become
> aware that while I can will the lie, I can by no
> means will that lying should be a universal law.
> For with such a law there would be no promises
> at all, since it would be in vain to allege my
> intention in regard to my future actions to
> those who would not believe this allegation, or
> if they over-hastily did so, would pay me back
> in my own coin. Hence my maxim, as soon as
> it should be made a universal law, would
> necessarily destroy itself."

Kant illustrates his deontological ethic with
the following example: A man needs to borrow money

and cannot repay the loan but realizes that no one will lend him the money unless he promises to repay it by a definite date. If he tells a lie to secure the loan, however, it would entail a necessary contradiction, willing one thing for oneself and another for others. For if everyone's promises were "vain pretenses," then all promises would be self-defeating and no one could believe any promise. Hence, one cannot will that lying to extricate oneself should become a universal law (Denise et al., section 11). Furthermore, the borrower would treat the lender as a mere means to an end, violating Kant's insistence that persons are ends in themselves.

Consider the following case in light of Kant's ethic.

THE CASE OF KATHERINE

Katherine, a freshman in high school, has an infatuation with Carl, a senior boy at the same school and a star on the football team. One Friday night after a home football game, Carl invites Katherine to an exclusive party at his house for football players, cheerleaders, and invited guests. Carl's parents are out-of-town, and Katherine enthusiastically accepts.

Everyone at the party is binge drinking, including Katherine, who wants to show Carl that she is mature and can fit in with his friends. Since

Katherine hasn't drunk much before, she quickly becomes inebriated and lies down on a bed. When Carl lies down next to her and kisses her, she doesn't protest. He proceeds to undress her, despite her physical though nonverbal resistance to sex; she attempts to push him away but does not say, "No."

The next day she tells her mom that she thinks she was "date raped."

➤ Do you agree or disagree, and why?

➤ How would Kant respond?

The Christian theologian and martyr Dietrich Bonhoeffer (1906-45), who has some sympathy for deontology but departs from ten Boom and Kant's absolute constraint never to lie, raises the issue whether the truth is due someone. He claims it is cynical "'to speak the truth' at all times and in all places to all men in the same way" (Bonhoeffer, 365). For example, a teacher asks a young boy in class whether his father is a drunkard. The boy lies and denies the charge against his father. Although an experienced person could question the teacher's presumptuousness and thus avoid telling a lie, the young boy acted responsibly and the teacher acted irresponsibly (ibid., 367f.). "From the principle of truthfulness," Bonhoeffer reasons,

> Kant draws the grotesque conclusion that I must even return an honest 'yes' to the enquiry of the murderer who breaks into my house and asks whether my friend whom he is pursuing has taken refuge there; in such a case self-righteousness of conscience has become outrageous presumption and blocks the path of responsible action. Responsibility is the total and realistic response of man to the claim of God and of our neighbor; but this example shows in its true light how the response of a conscience which is bound by principles is only a partial one. If I refuse to incur guilt against the principle of truthfulness for the sake of my friend, if I refuse to tell a robust lie for the sake of my friend (for it is only the self-righteously law-abiding conscience which will pretend that, in fact, no lie is involved), if, in other words, I refuse to bear guilt for charity's sake, then my action is in contradiction to my responsibility which has its foundation in reality (ibid., 245).

Consider the following case as Bonhoeffer's attempt to be responsible to his Jewish neighbors in Nazi Germany.

━━

THE CASE OF BONHOEFFER

Bonhoeffer wrestled with a responsible course of action when he considered joining the conspiracy to assassinate Hitler. As a pacifist committed to the principle of nonviolence, he thought it right to uphold the divine command, "Thou shall not murder" (New International Version). He also felt a duty not to be complicit in the state's killing of his Jewish neighbors. He could never justify participation in the plot to kill anyone, even Hitler, because Bonhoeffer believed that killing is always wrong (hence, his sympathy for deontology; however, he represented what ethicists have termed **divine command theory** or the belief that moral actions are based on duty or responsibility to God's commands, to be discussed in chapter four).

➢ Was there a "right" course of action for Bonhoeffer?

➢ Could God suspend his own command not to kill?

16

➤ What should Bonhoeffer do, and why?

~~~~~~

Consider the following case as a contemporary example of human rights and responsibilities, specifically of the church's response to gay rights.

~~~~~~

THE CASE OF FR. LOVEJOY

Fr. Lovejoy is a Roman Catholic priest that questions the church's adherence to traditional sexual mores, including the belief that genital sexual expression occurs only to express the mutual love of husband and wife. Fr. Lovejoy specifically disputes the church's traditional teaching that homosexual acts are "unnatural" as discernible by the natural light of reason, given that the order of nature dictates procreative relations between males and females to continue the human species. (Fr. Lovejoy

17

presupposes a belief in **natural law** or the theory of unchanging moral principles common to all people known by the natural light of reason.)

Fr. Lovejoy cites recent genetic studies to support his view that homosexual acts for some people are not "unnatural" but in fact quite "natural"—that is, in accordance with their constitutional predisposition to be attracted to members of the same sex. Fr. Lovejoy does insist that gay people, just like heterosexuals, restrict genital sexual expression to the context of monogamous loving relationships. To further that belief, he decides to marry a gay couple in his parish, so that they can express their sexual propensities within a permanent, committed relationship, calling this "holy union" of two men an event grounded in God's gracious love for all people over and against human bigotry.

While some parishioners support their priest's display of compassion and justice for disenfranchised gay couples and his desire to keep contemporary with scientific findings, others call for him to be defrocked for disobeying the church's official teaching and for disregarding the clear dictates of natural law.

➢ How would you deal with the tension between traditional sexual mores that reserve sexual intercourse for husband and wife and modern genetic studies that lend credence to gay rights advocates?

➤ How should the Roman Catholic Church respond to this iconoclastic priest, and why?

SUMMARY

Deontology upholds one's duty as intrinsically right and universally valid irrespective of goals, ends, or consequences. The ends do not justify the means; a "greater good" can never justify what is intrinsically wrong. **Divine command theory**—basing moral action on God's commands—also affirms duty over consequences and will be discussed more fully in chapter four. **Natural law** suggests unchanging moral principles common to all humans and discernible by the light of reason, thus showing its affinity for deontology as well.

➢ How would Kant respond to Bonhoeffer's conflict of duties both to follow God's command not to kill and to love his neighbors who were being killed in the name of all German citizens?

➢ How would Kant and Bonhoeffer advise Corrie ten Boom?

➢ How would they respond to the Fr. Lovejoy case?

Chapter Two: An Ethic of Consequences

Pleasure and the freedom from pain are the only things desirable as ends.

It is better to be a human being dissatisfied than a pig satisfied; better to be Socrates dissatisfied than a fool satisfied.

> ➤ John Stuart Mill

THE CASE OF GAIL AND HER BABY

Gail was 35, at work, and five months pregnant when her "water broke," signaling the imminent onset of labor. Considering the bleak odds of survival for a twenty-two week fetus, her doctor offered her an abortion. "You will probably give birth to a dead baby," he grimly informed her, "or a baby with very severe problems."

Opting for bed rest and drugs to delay labor, Gail and her baby fought the odds for nearly two weeks, after which time the chance of survival increased from ten to fifty percent—although the chance for blindness, cerebral palsy, or mental retardation were still high at twenty-four weeks of pregnancy.

Suddenly the baby went into cardiac distress. Another unpleasant dilemma: attempt delivery by C-section or wait for normal delivery, which would lessen the baby's chance of survival. The doctors disagreed. One calculated that the odds against having a live and healthy child were still significant and that surgery could complicate future pregnancies and risked a one in 50,000 chance of death for the mother. Given the risk to her, he stated that the choice was hers alone and not her husband's. The other doctor acknowledged these potential problems but insisted that a C-section provided the best chance for a live, healthy baby. She felt that the mother and father were morally obligated to maximize their baby's odds for survival and health, irrespective of the risks and difficulty of a C-section for the mother at twenty-four weeks. Gail had only moments to decide.

➤ What is the moral dilemma in this case?

➤ What are the relevant facts to resolving this dilemma?

22

➤ What convictions of the parents are relevant to their decision?

An ethic of consequences, usually termed **consequentialism** (or **teleology**), emphasizes the goals, ends, or consequences of an action in contrast with the deontologist's emphasis on the intrinsic rightness or wrongness of an action. The consequentialist argues that right action will maximize good results or that the ends justify the means. Rules are important to the consequentialist only as generalized statements of what promotes happiness in human experience (e.g., situation ethics' emphasis on the principle of love to discern what one should do in each situation). Experience teaches that one must often choose "the lesser of two evils." Varieties of consequentialism include **egoism** and **utilitarianism**.

Thomas Hobbes (1588-1679) defends **egoism** as the natural and reasonable right of self-interest and self-preservation over and against **altruism**, which prioritizes the interests of others. In fact, the right of self-preservation, he argues, includes the justification of all means necessary to preserve oneself. The natural state of humanity, prior to the creation of covenants or social bonds, pits one's self-interest against another's. Consider, for example, the implicit accusation against others when people lock their doors (Hobbes, section 5 in Denise et al.).

Primary source: Thomas Hobbes, *Leviathan*

"It may seem strange to some man, that has not well weighed these things; that nature should thus dissociate, and render man apt to invade, and destroy one another: and he may therefore, not trusting this inference, made from the passions, desire perhaps to have the same confirmed by experience. Let him therefore consider with himself, when taking a journey, he arms himself, and seeks to go well accompanied; when going to sleep, he locks his doors; when even in his house he locks his chests; and this when he knows there be laws, and public officers, armed, to revenge all injuries done to him; what opinion he has of his fellow subjects, when he rides armed; of his fellow citizens, when he locks his doors; and of his children, and servants, when he locks his chests. Does he not there as much accuse man's mankind by his actions, as I do by my words?"

John Stuart Mill (1806-73) presents **utilitarianism** as an attempt to move beyond the narrow individualistic self-interest of egoism while still advocating the pursuit of pleasure as the goal of morality for the larger society, hence being a form of altruism. Granting that we *do* pursue our own happiness (**individual psychological hedonism**), he argues that we *should* aim to achieve the best balance of pleasure over pain to maximize general happiness or the greatest good for the greatest number of people (**universal ethical hedonism**). "No reason can be given why the general happiness is desirable," writes Mill, "except that each person, so far as he believes it to be attainable, desires his own happiness" (Denise et al., sections 1, 2, 6, and 8). Whether or not it is clear why individuals should value general happiness, it is clear that Mill at least attempted to connect the individual pursuit of happiness to the well-being of others in society.

Primary source: John Stuart Mill, *Utilitarianism*

"The creed which accepts as the foundations of morals, Utility, or the Greatest Happiness Principle, holds that actions are right in proportion as they tend to promote happiness, wrong as they tend to promote unhappiness. By happiness is intended pleasure, and the absence of pain; by unhappiness, pain, and the privation of pleasure. . . . No reason can be given why the general happiness is desirable, except that each person, so far as he believes it to be attainable, desires his own happiness. This, however, being a fact, we have not only all the proof which the case admits of, but all which it is possible to require, that happiness is a good: that each person's happiness is a good to that person, and the general happiness, therefore, a good to the aggregate of all persons.

Consider the following case studies to illustrate the traditions of **egoism** and **utilitarianism**.

THE CASE OF LORRAINE AND FRANK

Lorraine was married to Frank for seventeen years when she decided to divorce him. They had met as college students, and, after a short romance, they decided to marry. Frank enrolled full-time in a seminary while working part-time, and Lorraine worked full-time while working on a seminary degree on a part-time basis. Even though the stress of earning graduate degrees while working and raising two children took its toll on the newlyweds, they seemed to have a stable life together and survived their seminary experience. Frank now works as an administrator at a Christian college, and Lorraine is pursuing ordination as a minister. Their children are now adolescents.

Lorraine had often complained that her relationship with Frank was not as close and as intimate as she desired; he was less open and talkative than she, even though he was a warm and stable presence in their family life. She went into therapy, which encouraged her to get in touch with her feelings and to do what made her happy. A couple of years later, she decided that their marriage

26

was a bad fit. Informing Frank one day that he was
not her "soul mate," she declared her intention to
divorce him. During their divorce proceedings, she
aggressively fought for possessions and custody of
the children, but at times she also hinted that she
might want to reconcile with Frank.

➤ What is the moral dilemma in this case?

➤ What are the relevant facts in this case?

➤ Should Frank attempt to salvage his marriage or
  continue the legal battle to unravel the common
  threads of their life together?

➤ Which course of action would be egoistic or
  utilitarian on his part, and what would you
  recommend to him if he were your friend?

THE CASE OF ALLAN AND DIANE

Once "swingers," Allan and Diane surprised their family and friends when they announced that they were engaged to be married. At their engagement party, they further surprised their guests by announcing that they would practice an "open marriage," which is to say that they would not necessarily practice monogamy. When questioned whether or not they thought such openness could work within a committed relationship, they both said that extramarital sex would not negatively affect their personal relationship.

A few years and two babies later, Diane kicked Allan out of the house and filed for divorce after discovering that he was acting on their vow of practicing an open marriage. Allan was reportedly not only seeing another woman, but he also charged gifts for this woman to his wife's credit card. Allan responded that he was simply acting on their mutual openness to extramarital sex, and since he paid the bills, it did not matter whose credit card he used.

After their divorce, Diane also asked the police to pick up Allan and put him in jail overnight because he had missed a child support payment. Allan did not show up to work, was dismissed from work when his employer discovered that he was in jail, and became further delinquent on child support payments when he could not obtain a new job due to his criminal record.

A couple of years later, Allan became employed again, and Diane moved with their two children to another state. Missing his children, Allan flew every other weekend to stay with them and his ex-wife, in part because he missed them and in part because their children had been "acting out" since the divorce. Allan and Diane consider becoming remarried for the sake of the children.

➤ Is remarriage for the children's sake a good idea?

➤ If they get remarried, would they need to reconsider whether an open marriage is a good idea?

➤ How would egoistic vs. utilitarian perspectives affect the likely outcome of an attempted marital reconciliation?

➤ What do you think they should do, and why?

SUMMARY

Consequentialism emphasizes the good outcomes of an action, not merely the intrinsic rightness of an action. **Egoism** defends self-interest, **altruism** upholds the interests of others, and **utilitarianism** values the greatest good for the greatest number of people.

➤ How well can one calculate the future consequences of an action?

➤ Is it morally acceptable to calculate the benefits of the majority at the expense of the minority?

➤ How might Hobbes and Mill advise Gail and her husband?

➤ Frank and Lorraine?

➤ Allan and Diane?

[S]tates of character arise out of [similar] activities . . . . It makes no small difference, then, whether we form habits of one kind or of another from our very youth; it makes a very great difference, or rather all *the difference.*

> ➤ Aristotle

THE CASE OF JOE

Joe is a student at a prep school that admits students who are academically capable and who subscribe to its honor code, which prohibits lying, cheating, and stealing. The penalty for violating the honor code is suspension or expulsion.

Joe is not a popular student and suffers from low self-esteem. While he subscribes to the honor code, he is also concerned about fitting in with his peers. During an exam, he observes two students glancing toward his exam paper. The teacher suspects the two students of cheating, and she also observes Joe looking quizzically at them but then

31

quickly looking away when she makes eye contact with him.

Knowing Joe as an honest person, she asks him what he observed. Although his moral instinct leads him to tell the truth, his concern about the repercussions of informing on fellow students pressures him to say, "Nothing." The two students, aware that she talked with him after the exam, ask Joe what he was discussing with the teacher. Joe again replies, "Oh, nothing." They warn him that that had better be the case or they will tell everyone that Joe informs on fellow students, thus breaking the students' code of silence. The consequence for Joe, they warn him, would be a lonely and tortured existence for the rest of his high school days.

➤ Is Joe being responsible to his fellow students by observing the code of silence?

➤ To his school?

➤ To himself?

➤ Which ethical tradition does the school's honor code represent?

➢ Can an honor code promote or protect character? Why or why not?

➢ What should Joe do, and why?

An **ethic of virtue** emphasizes one's character: namely, who one is and not simply what one does. From this perspective, ethical reflection focuses on moral agents, not merely on moral actions—on *being* good, not simply on *doing* good. Whereas both **deontology** and **consequentialism** understand morality as deciding what to do, an emphasis on virtue, including motives, reasons, and intentions, views character as foundational to conduct.

Aristotle (384-322 B.C.E.) understood moral virtue as the rational person's capacity to steer between extremes; pursuing a course of moderation entails embracing the "golden mean" and avoiding both excess and deficiency. Moral virtue, he believed, is developed and perfected by habit. (Aristotle, sections 8-11 in Denise et al.)

> **Primary source**: Aristotle, *Nicomachean Ethics*
>
> "Virtue, then, is a state of character concerned with choice, lying in a mean, i.e., the mean relative to us, this being determined by a rational principle, and by that principle by which the man of practical wisdom would determine it. Now it is a mean between two vices, that which depends on excess and that which depends on defect; and again it is a mean because the vices respectively fall short of or exceed what is right in both passions and actions, while virtue both finds and chooses that which is intermediate."

Deontology and Consequentialism "seem to differ at almost every point"; however, what they have in common is "morality as deciding" (McClendon 3). Such "decisionist" ethics focus on moral quandaries in isolation from the history of moral selves, argues Hauerwas, separating the decision (whether based on duty or consequences) from who we are as persons (1983, 20f., 128f.). The abortion debate, from this perspective, should not focus on the right of the mother vs. the right of the fetus, the circumstances of the pregnancy, or the abstract question of whether the fetus is a person. Instead, the abortion issue more fundamentally reveals the kind of people that we are and that we need to be. Inverting the statement, "no unwanted child ought ever to be born," Hauerwas asks a different question: What kind of people and communities do we need to be to welcome and hope for children (1981, 227ff.)?

An ethic of virtue indicates "a widespread dissatisfaction," argues Meilaender, with ethics that focus

> primarily on duties, obligations, troubling moral dilemmas, and borderline cases. Such cases are interesting, and certainly important when they arise, but we must admit that many of us go through long stretches of life in which we do not have to decide whether to frame one innocent man in order to save five, whether to lie to the secret police in order to hide someone, whether to approve aborting the ninth, possibly retarded, child of a woman whose husband has deserted her, and so forth. An ethic of virtue seeks to focus not only on such moments of great anxiety and uncertainty in life but also on the continuities, the habits of behavior which make us the persons we are. Not whether we should frame one innocent man to save five—but on the virtue of justice, with its steady, habitual determination to make space in life for the needs and claims of others. Not whether to lie to the secret police—but on that steady regard for others which uses language truthfully and thereby makes a common life possible. Not whether abortion is permissible in an extreme case—but on the ancient question which Socrates raised, whether it is better to suffer wrong than to do it. . . . *Being* not *doing* takes center stage; for what we ought to do may depend on the sort of person we are (4f.).

A truthful person who tells a lie, for example, is in better moral shape than a liar who tells the truth. The former has the character to recognize and rectify immoral behavior and the character to know when a lie might be appropriate, even though it harms the agent's character. The latter might no longer know the difference between a lie and the truth and would by sheer necessity have to tell the truth on occasion, if for no other reason than to be an effective liar!

Bonhoeffer counted the cost of compromising his character. He had learned how to deceive the Nazis, but he questioned whether he and others would have the character to help lead a post-Nazi Germany toward becoming a more virtuous nation. "Are we still serviceable?" Bonhoeffer questioned himself: "Will our spiritual resources prove adequate and our candor with ourselves remorseless enough to enable us to find our way back again to simplicity and straightforwardness?" (Bonhoeffer quoted in ibid., 10).

Try to determine which ethical traditions the characters implicitly assume or represent in the following cases.

THE CASE OF UNCLE CHARLIE

Charlie lives with his niece, her husband, and their two sons. Charlie's niece and her husband both work full-time in addition to caring for their two sons, one being severely psychologically afflicted and the other being a moderate to late stage alcoholic. Charlie is paralyzed and bedridden after suffering from a stroke, cancer, and a heart attack. He requires nursing help while his niece is at work, and his niece cares for him when she comes home from work.

Charlie's physician, Dr. Q, suggests that Charlie only has a few months, possibly weeks, to live. He offers Charlie and the family the option of euthanasia, since Charlie's short, painful time will lack the quality of life that persons normally enjoy. He lies in bed twenty-four hours a day and cannot move, eat, or eliminate without help; his medical care and treatment are also costly. His niece's husband objects to Dr. Q's implication that Uncle Charlie has somehow passed from being a person to a non-person. The niece, who is less interested in the philosophical discussion of what constitutes a person, exclaims, "My Uncle Charlie is not much of a person but he is still my Uncle Charlie" (quote borrowed from Hauerwas, 1977, 127ff.).

➢ Which ethical tradition does the doctor represent?

➢ Which traditions do the niece and her husband represent?

➤ What does it mean to be a person?

➤ How should the niece reconcile her love for her uncle and her other family responsibilities?

THE CASE OF MARY

In a discussion with her friends Sue and Laura, Mary confides to them that she is four months pregnant. Mary is a senior at a prep school. Because she is an honors student and the captain of the chess team, the community considers her one of its model citizens. Her parents especially have high expectations for her to succeed. Terrified that "my parents will kill me," embarrassed at the thought of appearing pregnant at graduation, and concerned about her college and career plans, she tells her friends that she needs to make a decision about having an abortion, and she needs to decide soon.

Laura cannot hold back her belief that abortion is killing innocent life and that Mary should be concerned about her baby more than herself. "What if all expectant mothers aborted their children?" she pointedly asks. Sue counters that a pregnancy will not only embarrass Mary, her parents, and her church but also will jeopardize Mary's future. Sue does not hold back her feeling that an abortion would remedy Mary's problem. Mary is torn between her friends, ashamed of her condition, and afraid that she will regret whichever course of action she takes.

➤ Which ethical tradition does each girl represent?

➤ What do you think Mary should do, and why?

SUMMARY

An **ethic of virtue** emphasizes persons over decisions. In fact, this tradition assumes a person of character will make virtuous decisions. Doing good is secondary to being good because moral acts reveal moral agency (including motives, reasons, and intentions). Good conduct presupposes good character.

➢ Which is foundational: conduct or character, and why?

➢ What would a virtue ethicist say to Joe?

➢ To Uncle Charlie's niece?

➢ To Mary?

*From what God does **for** us, we infer what God wants **with** us and **from** us.*

Decision does not lie in deciding the question whether this or that is the good, whether the command wants this or that of me, whether I should do this or that. An ethics which asks questions like this makes no more sense than a dogmatics which asks whether there is a God. The question to be decided in moral decision is whether I will be found obedient or disobedient in my action when confronted with the command at its most concrete and specific.

➢ Karl Barth

THE CASE OF BARTH

Karl Barth (1886-1968), a professor of theology at the University of Bonn, contemplated the plight of the Jews and his own fate when Hitler and the National Socialists seized power in 1933. Barth had earlier "characterized Fascism as a religion, 'with its deep-rooted, dogmatic ideas about one thing, national reality, its appeal to foundations which are not foundations at all, and its emergence as sheer power'" (quoted in Busch, 218). With Hitler as the new Chancellor in Germany, Barth immediately and instinctively knew that "my dear German people were beginning to worship a false God" (ibid., 223).

Barth vehemently opposed the so-called "German Christians" and accused them of breaking the First Commandment to have no other gods before God. Barth led the representatives of the Confessing Church, gathered at Barmen in 1934, to call the Church to confess Jesus Christ as "the one Word of God, whom we are to hear, whom we are to trust and obey in life and death" and to condemn the false teaching of the German Christians that perverted the Gospel by attempting to wed it with a political ideology that worshipped "another lord" (Barmen in Leith, 517ff.).

When Hitler required that all officials give him the oath of loyalty—"Heil, Hitler!" (*Heil* literally means "holy")—Barth realized that beginning his classes with this obligatory oath would compromise his faith in the sole Lordship of Christ. If he refused, however, he would be dismissed from his university position, expelled from Germany, and removed from the struggle to overcome Hitler. As Barth entered class, his fate and participation in this critical moment in German history were at stake.

➢ Could Barth reconcile his unequivocal statement at Barmen with giving the oath for the sake of remaining in Germany to participate in the bigger battle or must he make his own confession of faith without regard for the consequences to demonstrate his loyalty to the one true Lord?

➢ What should he do, and why?

※※※※※※※※※※※※※※※※※※※※※※※※※※※※※※※※※※※※

Whereas the ethic of virtue thinkers challenge the traditional distinction between deontology and consequentialism as merely flip sides of the same coin (or as two different forms of "decisionism"), **divine command** theorists such as Karl Barth and Dietrich Bonhoeffer challenge the whole western ethical enterprise as an autonomous attempt to defy God's commands and create moral laws by and for oneself. A philosophical ethic, they argue, starts with the question, "How can I do good?" (deontology and consequentialism) or, "How can I be good?" (ethic of virtue). Both questions, however, presuppose that the starting point for ethics is the self, rather than the basis of a theological ethic: namely, God and his commands.

"Whoever wishes to take up the problem of a Christian ethics must be confronted at once with a demand which is quite without parallel. He must from the outset discard as irrelevant the two questions which alone impel him to concern himself with the problem of ethics, 'How can I be good?' and 'How can I do good?', and instead of these he must ask the utterly and totally different question 'What is the will of God?' This requirement is so immensely far-reaching because it presupposes a decision with regard to the ultimate reality; it presupposes a decision of faith. If the ethical problem presents itself essentially in the form of enquiries about one's own being good and doing good, this means that it has already been decided that it is the self and the world which are the ultimate reality. The aim of all ethical reflection is, then, that I myself shall be good and that the world shall become good through my action. But the problem of ethics at once assumes a new aspect if it becomes apparent that these realities, myself and the world, themselves lie embedded in a quite different ultimate reality, namely, the reality of God, the Creator, Reconciler and Redeemer. What is of ultimate importance is now no longer that I should become good, or that the condition of the world be made better by my action, but that the reality of God should show itself everywhere to be the ultimate reality."

Whether one starts with abstract, immutable law (deontology), changing situations and circumstances (consequentialism), or character (ethic of virtue), the attempt to root goodness in oneself apart from God is the essence of sin. Consider how the fallen human attempt to discern between good and evil—"the fruit of the tree was good for food" (Gen. 3:6)—betrayed the sinful human attempt to construct an abstract moral criterion independent of God's concrete command not to "eat from the tree of the knowledge of good and evil" (Gen. 2:17). God had given freedom to the primal human pair to eat from any other tree in the garden (Gen. 2:16)—and likewise perhaps a freedom to engage in ethical deliberation. But the original sin that Adam and Eve committed presupposed an *autonomy* to discern for oneself good and evil, even in direct opposition to God's commands. Sin both disrupted their relationship with God and with one another (Adam lording over Eve [Gen. 3:16] and Cain killing his brother Abel [Gen. 4:8] being two immediate examples of the disrupting impact of sin upon human relationships).

> From this moment on we are caught up in a very strange venture! For the very act by which man wants to decide what is good, wants to know the good by himself, constitutes the sin. Thus, sin is not the failure to obey a morality. It is the very desire to determine that morality independently of God, a desire which is, at the same time, concupiscence, the will to power. Consequently, the most virtuous man who at the cost of prolonged asceticism cries, 'There is

the good,' is the very one who reproduces for each person, and in each person, the sin of Adam (Ellul, 13).

Relationship with God, continues Jacques Ellul (French sociologist and theological ethicist who writes in the tradition of Barth and Bonhoeffer), is the only basis for knowing and doing God's will. All else, including morality and religion as human enterprises, is nothing short of idolatry (ibid., 16ff.).

God's grace, according to the Bible, is the basis for proper relations with God, others, oneself, and creation. The Ten Commandments, for example, begin with the proclamation, "I am the Lord your God, who brought you out of Egypt, out of the land of slavery" (Ex. 20:2). Therefore, "You shall have no other gods before me" (v. 3). The other commands that follow are obligations to the covenant God of Israel, not legal stipulations of a contract. God's love, not merely his law, obligates humanity to live responsibly with God, others, oneself, and creation. "I am your God, and you shall be my people," a key refrain of the Hebrew Scriptures, is not merely a command, but also a promise: You *shall* be my people. God unconditionally binds himself to Israel and promises to uphold and fulfill his covenant with Israel on behalf of humanity. For Barth, Bonhoeffer, and Ellul, God's promise to Israel is fulfilled by the Jewish man Jesus on behalf of all people, whether they be Jew or Gentile, male or female, rich or poor, slave or free.

THE CASE OF JOHN

After serving over ten years in prison, John is facing his parole board for the first time since his rape conviction and subsequent attempted escape from prison. He appears remorseful and confesses to being a new person in Christ. Acknowledging the large number of "repentant" convicts, he nonetheless insists that his recent conversion is genuine and has provided him with insight into his past behavior. Claiming to be a victim of alcohol and other drug abuse, he admits that he had become a predator, one who had raped a sophomore girl in high school to whom he felt attracted and who was five years younger than he. Expressing shame and guilt for the brutality of his crime—although he finds a small measure of consolation for not harming her beyond what he describes as the viciousness of the crime itself—he believes that he has paid his debt to society. Confident that Jesus has forgiven him and will prevent him from returning to his self-centered, manipulative lifestyle and aware that his victim and he will never forget the horror of his crime, he presents himself as reformed and renewed.

➤ Should he be released on parole based on his testimony?

> How would you evaluate his parole request from the perspective of each of the four ethical traditions?

THE CASE OF CAMERON

Cameron is single and likely celibate for life. He has not taken a vow of celibacy; rather, his idealistic expectations for a wife often prevent him from cultivating relationships with actual women. Since Cameron is in his forties, the odds for fulfilling his dreams for a wife and children are diminishing.

Cameron teaches at a church-related college. Lisa, one of his faculty colleagues, tells him that she is divorcing her husband, whom she found in bed with another woman. Given her husband's history of affairs with multiple partners, she is also concerned that her husband—and thus she—might be HIV positive. She informs Cameron that she is suing her husband for sole custody of their three children, who are six, nine, and thirteen years old.

Cameron tentatively pursues a dating relationship with Lisa, struggling with his desires for marriage and especially for children of his own.

Although Lisa reciprocates romantic interest in Cameron, she is beyond her child-bearing years and already has three children. The lingering emotional effects of her divorce also pose an obstacle to developing a commitment to one another. Their common vacillation finally overcomes their mutual attraction, and they break off their relationship.

While Cameron wistfully considers what might have been, if only Lisa were younger and not marred by her circumstances, he soon discovers that she is dating another faculty colleague at their school—a *married* faculty colleague. Lisa is not only committing adultery, but she is also conducting her affair on-campus (after school hours). Cameron is aware of his personal feelings of pain, but he cannot set aside that her behavior offends the school community. Students are aware of the adulterous affair, which violates the school's Judeo-Christian heritage.

Cameron decides to report his adulterous colleagues to the Dean of the Faculty. Cameron demands that the Dean uphold the school's statement of faith, which specifies allegiance to the moral and spiritual precepts of the Bible. Since adultery breaks one of the Ten Commandments and undermines the faculty pledge to serve as positive role models for students, Cameron demands that the Dean fire his two colleagues.

➢ If you were the Dean of the Faculty at this loosely church-affiliated college, how would you respond to this situation?

➤ Can professors at such a college validly divorce their personal and professional ethics? (Consider this question for other positions as well, such as high school teachers, educational administrators, or government officials.)

THE CASE OF WHITNIÉ AND DANIEL

Whitnié and Daniel are in their early 20's and first-year graduate students in a marriage and family therapy program. Their initial attraction to each other leads to a dating relationship, though they soon realize how different they are: she grew up in an affluent neighborhood, and he grew up poor; she is an optimist, and he is a cynic. They even hold different attitudes on points where they agree—for example, they both believe in God, but he questions his faith, and she takes such matters for granted.

On one date, they attempt to clarify the nature of their relationship. They discuss their points of compatibility and difference, and, despite acknowledging their divergent outlooks on life, they agree that they appreciate and enjoy each other enough to continue dating. A little over a year later, they are married.

Their first year of marriage, not surprisingly, is filled with tensions. Whitnié enjoys acquiring expensive possessions, for example, and Daniel prefers a frugal, Spartan existence. Personal habits become points of conflict, too, such as Daniel's propensity to snore and to watch ballgame after ballgame on TV while Whitnié is doing the housework.

After six years of marriage and many counseling sessions, Whitnié announces one day that she is moving out of the house, and she is unsure whether she will return. "We're just not a good fit," she tells Daniel, "and I need time to sort things out." He protests that they knew of their incompatibility early on in their dating relationship but still decided that the good outweighed the bad when they married each other. She does not relent, moves into an apartment, and eventually begins to develop relationships with other men.

Daniel continues to pursue Whitnié, communicate more openly about their relational problems, and hope that they can effect a reconciliation. One evening, after going on a date together, Whitnié tells Daniel that she has felt much better about their recent time together, but the next day she communicates her fear to him that their relationship would again deteriorate. "So have you decided to pursue a divorce?" he asks her nearly six months after she has moved out. Her reply is quick and icy, "Yes."

Their divorce papers indicate that they will be terminating their marriage because of "irreconcilable differences." Daniel strongly believes that marriage is a lifelong commitment and that their differences, although real, are reconcilable. Some friends, Lisa and Natalia, urge him to wait and pray, citing Jesus' teaching on divorce that "anyone who divorces his wife, except for marital unfaithfulness, causes her to become an adulteress, and anyone who marries the divorced woman commits adultery" (Mt. 5:32). Other friends see matters differently. Kim bluntly suggests, "Forget about her, and start seeing other women." Maria, who has had an eye on Daniel for some time, invites him over for homemade pizza and "a shoulder to cry on."

➢ Should he sign the divorce decree or are there other alternatives that he should consider?

➢ Does Jesus' teaching against divorce apply to him or would he be justified in acquiescing to the divorce?

➢ If he does acquiesce, would he be morally and spiritually freed from his marital commitment to consider dating and remarriage, and at what point?

SUMMARY

God's commands, not merely human attempts to be ethical, are the focus of **divine command theory**. Even an emphasis on human virtue or religion can be a disguised attempt of humans to rebel against God and his commands, setting up independent standards apart from God.

➢ Does this tradition challenge your ethical system? How so or why not?

➢ Does human autonomy represent original sin? Why or why not?

➢ How might Barth respond to the cases of John and Cameron?

Part Two:

Moral Reasoning

The cultivation of the mind is a kind of food supplied for the soul of man.

> ➢ Cicero

A fact-opinion dichotomy often governs ethical discussions, the assumption being that ethical opinions or confessions of belief are the alternative to facts or empirically verifiable statements. **Moral relativism**, for example, suggests that since moral values vary among persons and cultures, conflicting value judgments or opinions can be equally valid. **Emotivism**, likewise, asserts that ethical statements are merely feelings that can only be vented or imposed on others. Ethical assertions, in these popular views, do not essentially differ from expressing one's preference for flavors of ice cream or brands of pizza.

The assumption of this book is that one can and should offer reasoned arguments to support one's opinions and that *some* issues are not debatable. In addition to developing awareness of the implicit ethical traditions that govern ethical discussions, developing reasoned arguments for one's moral judgments is both possible and desirable in the quest for moral truth. While no one should simply assert his or her view as absolute truth, questions of freedom, justice, and dignity weigh too heavily on the human scale to be relegated to the mere status of personal opinion. What moral language can be conjured up by those who deny that there are *some* universal rights and wrongs to denounce as intolerable, for example, a society's permitting slavery, rape, child abuse, murder, or genocide?

In developing an argument and defending a position, one should

> ➢ *clearly* state his or her position;

> ➢ *consistently* adhere to this position within a paper or for the duration of the debate;

> ➢ *coherently* develop the position so that it forms a unified and orderly pattern of thought (developing one's position with a conscious reliance on an ethical tradition should help here); and

> ➢ *cogently* or persuasively defend all assertions.

The reader should have no difficulty understanding the position or tracing clear steps from the premises to conclusions. Even those who disagree with the conclusions should be able to understand why someone supports that position and how one arrived at the conclusions.

One should specifically avoid the following logical fallacies or errors of thought during ethical debates:

Begging the question: assuming or asserting one's view as true without providing support for one's claim. "Pro-life" and "pro-choice" labels, for example, reveal attempts to beg the question whether fetal life deserves legal protection or whether mothers should have the choice to abort fetal life. The debate usually hinges on whether or not the fetus is a person and, therefore, does or does not deserve legal protection.

Non sequitur: asserting a conclusion that does not follow from one's premises. The creation vs. evolution debate, although not an ethical issue (for most people at least), illustrates this fallacy: "Evolution is true; therefore, God does not exist" or "The Bible is true; therefore, evolution is wrong." In both cases, the conclusion does not follow from the premises.

Ad hominem: attacking the person instead of evaluating his or her argument—e.g., calling defenders of abortion rights "murderers" or opponents of abortion rights "fanatics." These terms also illustrate the fallacy of using **loaded language** or emotionally laden words.

Genetic fallacy: labeling the source of an idea, rather than evaluating its substance—e.g., "That's a liberal Democratic proposal" or "That's the religious right's agenda."

Straw man: attacking a caricature of your opponent's position—e.g., portraying proponents or opponents of abortion rights as "extremists" that permit no exceptions to their position, even though they do permit exceptions to their position.

False dilemma: assuming simple black/white, either/or options—e.g., "pro-life" or "pro-choice"—as if nuance were unattainable or untenable.

Doubtful cause (or **post hoc, ergo propter hoc**: lit. "after this, therefore because of this"): assuming a statistical correlation implies causation. If a state institutes the death penalty, for example, and the murder rate goes down, it is fallacious to assume that the death penalty caused the decrease in the murder rate. Other factors or variables might have been contributing factors (such as increased police funding) or the murder rate might have declined anyway. Inability to control such factors makes it difficult to establish a causal pattern.

Equivocation: failing to take a stand on an issue. Advocates for a moderate position in a debate often mistakenly assume the role of "fence-sitting" instead of defending a distinct position between the pro and con positions. An open mind should not reveal an empty head.

Hasty generalization: drawing conclusions based on insufficient evidence, especially to confirm one's *a priori* beliefs or mindset. "I knew a welfare cheat in New Jersey," for example, is proffered as proof that welfare recipients routinely abuse the system.

Overstatement: using words that suggest absolute and universal truth—e.g., "always" or "never." Instead of these unrealistic claims, use qualifiers such as "generally" or "tends."

False use of authority: appealing to expertise or sacred sources without adequate support—e.g., "Scientists say . . ." or "The Bible says . . . ." Also, be suspicious of sources with vested interests—e.g., National Rifle Association statistics on gun use and control or National Organization of Women statistics on abortion.

Bad analogy: drawing weak comparisons or ignoring important differences. Consider, for example, whether or not the traditional abortion rights analogy is a good one—namely, that a fetus is no more a person than an acorn is a tree.

Researching standard arguments and defenses of positions will help students see how significant thinkers have developed their ethical arguments. Good student papers should show evidence both of careful, empathic reading of important sources and of critical synthesis of these sources, so that students restate in their words these basic ideas and arguments. Documentation of ideas—both quotations and paraphrased ideas—is, of course, essential to give credit to authors for their ideas and phrases and to give credit to oneself for careful research, so include internal (or parenthetical) documentation and a bibliography of sources cited or consulted.

SUMMARY

➤ Develop and defend one's position and ethical tradition clearly, consistently, coherently, and cogently.

➤ Avoid logical fallacies.

➤ Research standard arguments and document sources in papers to defend one's position in formal debate.

CONCLUSION

Why be a moral person? Deontologists appeal to duty, arguing that respect for universal rules will make the world a just place in which to live. Consequentialists consider the consequences, assuming that grappling with the outcomes of one's actions will create a more loving and humane world. Virtue ethicists emphasize one's character as foundational to conduct, believing that virtuous people will make good decisions and that pondering bizarre moral quandaries does not necessarily advance virtue. Divine command theologians believe that both virtue and vice reveal sinful human attempts to know the difference between good and evil, so that human autonomy supplants obedience to God's commands.

Whether or not one agrees that God's commands are foundational for ethics (and ample empirical evidence exists to support the claim that one can be moral without God), the title of this book at least indicates a bias towards valuing virtue in matters of ethical decision-making and daily living. God commands, after all, that we be moral people. A person of character will have the moral instincts to know what to do in the innumerable situations of life and will have the moral sense to know when he or she needs forgiveness and repentance. This points to a further bias, which is that divine command theory complements ethic of virtue theory. For even the virtuous need God's commands and words of forgiveness and reconciliation, whether for lapses of good character or for pride in good character!

Although clear, consistent, coherent, and cogent arguments are essential for the ethical enterprise, in the final analysis, the world needs more than good thinkers and debaters. People who have the character to know and do what is right—or at least what is responsible—are the kinds of people that I want to surround me when I face both the moral dilemmas on the boundaries of life and the ordinary task and gift of being human in the midst of everyday life. If this slim volume has contributed in any way to thinking about ethics not only as an academic exercise but also as a foundational personal question—namely, who am I as a person and what kind of life do I wish to live in my relationships with others?—then it has satisfied the original question with which we began, "Why write another book?"

BIBLIOGRAPHY

Barth, Karl. *Ethics*. Ed. Dietrich Braun & trans. Geoffrey W. Bromiley. New York: Seabury, 1981.

Bonhoeffer, Dietrich. *Ethics*. Ed. Eberhard Bethge & Trans. Neville Horton Smith. New York: Collier/Macmillan, 1955.

Busch, Eberhard. *Karl Barth: His Life from Letters And Autobiographical Texts*. Trans. John Bowden. Phila.: Fortress, 1975.

Denise, Theodore C. & Peterfreund, Sheldon P. *Great Traditions in Ethics* (7th ed.). Belmont, CA: Wadsworth, 1992.

Ellul, Jacques. *To Will and To Do*. Trans. C. Edward Hopkin. Phila.: Pilgrim, 1969.

Frankena, William K. *Ethics*. Englewood Cliffs, NJ: 1963.

Giardina, Denise. *Saints and Villains: A Novel*. New York: W. W. Norton, 1998.

Glazener, Mary. *The Cup of Wrath: The Story of Dietrich Bonhoeffer's Resistance to Hitler*. Savannah: Frederic C. Beil, 1992.

Hauerwas, Stanley. *The Peaceable Kingdom: A Primer In Christian Ethics.*   Notre Dame, IN: Notre Dame Press, 1983.

_____. *Truthfulness and Tragedy: Further Investigations in Christian Ethics.*   Notre Dame, IN: Notre Dame Press, 1977.

Holmes, Arthur F. *Ethics.* Downers Grove, IL: InterVarsity, 1984.

Leith, John H., ed. *Creeds of the Churches*, rev. ed. Richmond: John Knox, 1973.

McBrien, Richard P. *Catholicism: Study Edition.* San Francisco: Harper & Row, 1981.

McClendon, Jr., James Wm. *Ethics: Systematic Theology,* Vol.1. Nashville: Abingdon, 1986.

Meilaender, Gilbert C. *The Theory and Practice of Virtue.*   Notre Dame, IN: Notre Dame Press, 1984.

Rachels, James. *The Elements of Moral Philosophy* . 2nd ed. New York: McGraw-Hill, 1993.

_____. *The Right Thing To Do: Basic Readings in Moral Philosophy.*   New York: McGraw-Hill, 1989.

Sommers, Christina Hoff. *Right and Wrong: Basic*

Readings in Ethics. Fort Worth: Harcourt Brace, 1986.

Sommers, Christina, & Fred Sommers. *Vice & Virtue In Everyday Life: Introductory Readings in Ethics.* 4th ed. Fort Worth: Harcourt Brace, 1997.

APPENDIX

Webb School of Knoxville students Jennifer Birk, Anna Marie Carlson, Katherine Duckett, Rachel Dunaway, Rissa Ivens, Nick Panella, Sarah Peeden, and Kati Sanford wrote or edited the following case studies and discussions of issues. Their keen and careful work will benefit future students who read and discuss these materials, and I am indebted to them for the considerable time and dedication that they contributed to this project.

Each "Framing the Issue" section is preceded by a case situation and is based on the introductory materials by Prof. Lawrence Hinman in his *Contemporary Moral Issues: Diversity and Consensus* (Upper Saddle River, NJ: Prentice Hall, 2000), 2nd ed.

Abortion: The Case of Lucy's Baby

Lucy is a fifteen-year-old who does well in school and is a varsity basketball player. Her parents go to church often, and sometimes she goes with them. Their conservative values oppose abortion and premarital sex, but Lucy rejects their values, hates her home, and focuses only on basketball and her boyfriend.

Will is her boyfriend, and she thinks that she is in love with him. One night at his house, they decide to have sex. Lucy does not regret this decision until two months later. She starts noticing that she is sick in the morning and that she has skipped two periods. She becomes panicked when she gets a positive result from an over-the-counter pregnancy test. Her head racing with thoughts, she tries to calm down and decide what to do. She calls Will and tells him the situation, and he claims that the baby does not belong to him. Lucy is now faced with the decision of what to do.

> Should Lucy tell her parents about the baby? Should Lucy have an abortion?

Framing the Issue: Abortion

Before one can begin to examine the greater moral issues and questions facing the world today, one must first focus on the most fundamental human concern: birth. The debate over abortion has raged throughout our society, with its principal divisions being "pro-life" and "pro-choice." These two groups tend to focus on separate and specific points of the abortion issue; namely, pro-life advocates argue for the rights of the unborn, while pro-choice advocates emphasize the rights of the pregnant woman.

A major issue in the abortion debate is whether or not the fetus is actually a person, and, if it is, what rights it possesses. As evidenced by the division between the pro-life and pro-choice viewpoints, when the rights of two beings (even potential beings) are involved, the issue becomes far more complicated. Efforts have been made to specify just what determines personhood; however, so far no uniform criterion has been established. A few suggestions include the conceived by humans criterion, the physical resemblance criterion, the future-like-ours criterion, the genetic structure argument, and the viability argument. The nature of these arguments can be largely determined from their categorization. Obviously, the conceived by humans criterion means that a fetus is considered a person if it is conceived by humans while the future-like-ours criterion maintains that the potential life the fetus might lead qualifies it as a person. Though each has its merits, none have been successful in convincing society that the fetus is or is not a person.

Some have chosen to disregard the issue completely. Judith Jarvis Thompson, who wrote "A Defense of Abortion," was the first individual to suggest that "personhood" does not necessarily mean "right to life." While this is a highly controversial argument, many have come to accept this idea as a valid viewpoint. The main question is one that will recur through many moral issues: does a right to life entitle one to infringe on the rights of another? The rights of pregnant women have been broken down into four main categories: the right to privacy, the right to ownership and control over one's body, the right to equal treatment, and the right to self-determination. While all of these rights are important for any individual, there is a question of whether a woman who becomes pregnant sacrifices some of these rights.

Many moderates suggest that abortion should be legal only in extreme cases: rape, incest, et cetera.

However, many women's rights activists argue that no matter what the situation, a woman's body is her own, and the government does not have a right to decide what she chooses to do with it. As you can understand, it is extremely difficult to determine who has rights, what these rights are, and where they end. This is the main obstacle in resolving the abortion issue, an obstacle that has divided many for years. Furthermore, there is one other individual involved whose rights are not so carefully considered: the father. Of course, a woman carries the physical burden of pregnancy and birth, but the father, especially if he is a spouse, is likely to be involved in the child's future. His rights, though not as pressing as those of the mother or the fetus, present another problem in settling this issue.

Yet another way to view this situation is from a utilitarian perspective. Abortions occur because of unwanted pregnancies, which lead to overpopulation and the possible abuse and neglect of children. Society has generally tried to prevent these pregnancies through promoting the values of abstinence and chastity, but, in a changing world, some have argued that these measures may not be sufficient. They suggest that because unwanted pregnancies are an ever-present problem, society should devise the means to deal with their effects. Abortion is one way to eliminate unwanted pregnancies, or rather, unwanted births.

As with any moral issue, all these views have their merits and weaknesses. While many take abortion as a deeply personal issue, it is important to carefully consider and debate all viewpoints.

Questions:
1) Is the question of whether or not the fetus is a person essential to the abortion argument?

2) When do you think a fetus or unborn child obtains the right to life?

3) In what ways can the personhood line be redesigned to a point that is less arbitrary than it is now? In what ways could the pro-choice and pro-life views meet on a middle ground?

4) What do you consider a just cause of self-determination to have an abortion?

5) What role, if any, should the father have in deciding whether the mother should have an abortion?

6) Are there other ways to deal with unwanted births without having to resort to abortion?

Surrogate Motherhood:
The Case of Jack and Shirley

Jack and Shirley are a middle aged couple who are faced with the inability to have children. While they are not extremely wealthy, they have spent thousands of dollars trying to have children of their own. Finally, they are left with only two options:

adopt, or enlist the aid of a surrogate mother. The adoption process is lengthy and uncertain, and the child would not be biologically theirs, so Jack and Shirley opt to try and find a surrogate mother.

Without much trouble, one of their close friends, Julie, decides that she is willing to become the surrogate mother for the couple. It is agreed that Jack's sperm and Julie's egg will be used because Shirley is infertile. Because it is between friends, there is no written agreement between the three, yet Jack and Shirley will pay for the medical expenses and also pay Julie for the use of her egg and uterus.

Julie is soon impregnated with Jack's sperm and after an uneventful pregnancy a baby boy is born. However, after giving birth, Julie decides that she cannot give up the baby. She claims that since she is the biological and gestational mother and the fact that there is no binding legal contract, the child is hers.

> ➤ Who are the real parents? Who deserves custody over the child?

Framing the Issue: Reproductive Technologies

Babies created in glass dishes. Exact human replicas made from cells of existing human beings. Genetic manipulation of embryos in the womb. These processes sound like the stuff of science fiction; a few chapters out of a book predicting an unrealistic future. But these are not technologies of the future—they are today's technologies, our creations. In the last section, the discussion focused mainly on what the rules are when one is faced with an "unwanted baby." In this section, the focus changes to what one must consider when someone desperately wants to have a baby, resorting to these unconventional technologies to have that child.

There are several options for parents who, because of infertility or other problems, cannot have a child on their own. These include in vitro fertilization, artificial insemination by donor, and surrogacy. The simplest method is artificial insemination by donor (AID), which is only effective in cases of male infertility. In vitro fertilization involves a doctor combining the sperm and egg of the parents in a glass dish and then implanting the created embryo into the mother's womb. The case, however, is not always this simple. The egg and sperm may not always be those of the intending parents (the couple who wishes to have the baby) or the embryo may be implanted in a surrogate, who will then bear the child.

While these ideas, from a scientific standpoint, sound fairly reasonable, the fact remains that these technological advancements interfere with nature and human emotions. From a societal point of view, we must examine what effect these developments will have upon our world. Many object to in vitro fertilization because the process creates hundreds of pre-embryos that are later discarded. As with the abortion debate, the question of whether or not the pre-embryo is a person is a major factor in this issue. There are also broader issues at play here. Many religious thinkers strongly object to reproductive technologies because they are, in a way, "playing God." They argue that we cannot control our destinies, and that our fates are ultimately in the hands of the divine. Religious philosophers are not the only ones who oppose the use of this technology, however. Many feel that separating sexual intercourse from human reproduction is an unnatural and potentially harmful action. It is difficult and somewhat frightening to predict what effect separating sex, a natural act of love, from conception will have on our society. In addition, we must determine if paying a woman to carry a child is immoral or detrimental to women.

On a more personal level, we can first examine what sort of effect these technologies will have on the child they create. Since the parents who raise the child may not be their genetic or birth parents, the child may feel isolated or confused when he or she learns of this. Struggling with problems of identity, he or she may even go so far as to seek out his or her genetic or birth parents. The surrogate, or woman who carries and has the baby, may become attached to the child and change her mind about giving it up. Is this fair? Since she may be the genetic mother as well as the birth mother, does she have a claim on the child?

There are three ways one can view the relationship between the surrogate mother and the intentional parents: as a contract model, as an adoption model, or as a cooperative model. The contract model allows us to view the situation from a legal standpoint. The intentional parents and the surrogate mother enter into a lawful contract; therefore, each must deliver, as it were, what they agree to deliver. This model tends to overlook the emotional and personal aspects of the situation, and many argue that a "contract" is inappropriate because it involves "selling babies." The adoption model effectively deals with many of these problems. In this model, the surrogate mother has a specified period of time in which she can change her mind about giving up the baby. In addition, she receives no payment for the child, but may receive payment for living and medical costs. There are, however, problems in relating surrogacy to adoption. In adoption, the mother does not become pregnant for the intending parents; the pregnancy is, more often than not, unintentional. In adoption, the child has no genetic links to the intending parents; in surrogacy, there is always a genetic contribution from at least one parent. The final perspective, known as the cooperative model, allows the surrogate mother and intending parents to work together in deciding what they wish to gain from the relationship and making sure they attain that wish. The intending parents should not seek out a surrogate simply for superficial reasons (inconvenience of pregnancy to career, etc.), but only because they have a medical concern involving themselves or the baby. They should also choose a surrogate mother whose main motive is not money. While most surrogate mothers welcome the fee, they do not endure pregnancy just for payment. They may enjoy being pregnant or may feel obligated to help parents who cannot conceive a child.

With recent advances in technology, we find ourselves facing several options that will affect the future of our children. Children facing potentially life-threatening or debilitating diseases would benefit from genetic manipulation. It would most certainly give them a more normal life. However, there is a danger of this technology when used for other, less important means, such as changing eye color, hair color, gender, et cetera. If we choose to accept genetic manipulation as a valid technology, are we responsible for making sure it does not run rampant? Or should parents be allowed to choose the exact life and look they want for their child? Let us consider the effect of allowing parents to choose their children's gender. If more couples prefer male children to females, or vice versa, this could severely throw off the balance of society. It is potentially dangerous for diversity to allow these technologies to be used for non-medical purposes.

We are perfecting the technology to replicate humans, create babies, and change their future. It is our responsibility as a society to decide how these technologies affect our community and if their widespread use should even be allowed.

Questions:
1) Should a surrogate mother be able to change her mind and keep the baby? What rights does she have regarding the child?

2) Which model do you think best portrays how the relationship between the surrogate mother and the intended parents should be?

3) Should there be limits to who has access to

reproductive technologies? Should only sterile couples have access to them? Should the government regulate such access?

4) Should designer babies be banned, and if so, to what extent? Consider the benefits of controllng diseases and defects.

5) Should there be conditions that need to be met in order for a couple to choose the use of a surrogate mother? Is it okay to use a surrogate mother just to avoid the inconvenience of having a baby?

Euthanasia: The Case of Johnny's Life

Johnny was a twenty-five-year-old newlywed whose wife Jennifer had just become pregnant. Johnny and Jennifer had been high school sweethearts, and they continued dating throughout college and were married after graduation. He had recently started his first job as an architect. Jennifer and Johnny were adjusting to their new life, and they were in the process of buying a house big enough for their expanding family. Jennifer, who worked as a realtor, had found an affordable house in a good section of town that was close to Johnny's new office.

One day Jennifer was showing another couple a house when she received a phone call, which informed her that a tractor trailer had hit Johnny's car head on as he was leaving his work site. Johnny was rushed to the nearby hospital. When Jennifer arrived, Johnny's parents were waiting in the emergency room. The doctor showed them to the waiting room, and he informed them that as soon as he knew something he would let them know.

Finally, after a couple of hours, the doctor returned with the dreaded news: Johnny had suffered a severe blow to his head. At the moment, Johnny was essentially brain dead or in a vegetative state; he could no longer talk, eat, walk, or think. Unable to breathe, he was on a respirator. If he regained consciousness, the doctors hoped that he would be able to maintain at least some control over his muscles. However, he was only given a fifteen percent chance to come out of his present state.

The first option was to consider Johnny's wishes if he expressed them in a living will, but Jennifer informed them that he had not done so. The other option was to allow Jennifer, being his wife, to make the decision as to what should be done. Otherwise, the hospital was legally obligated to preserve his life. Johnny's parents thought that, since there is no point in continuing life just to keep the body alive, Johnny should be taken off the respirator and allowed a peaceful death; however, Jennifer wanted to wait until she had the baby, and the baby was old enough to remember its father. She also felt that Johnny's chance at living provided hope for the future.

➤ What should Jennifer do and why?

Framing the Issue: Euthanasia

In the last two sections, we dealt with life: when it begins, who is entitled to it, and how we may create it. In this section, we will focus on the opposite end of the spectrum: death. Euthanasia is often referred to as "mercy killing" and takes place when one wishes to die or when others decide that it would be better for that person to pass on. Naturally, the matter is rarely simple or clear-cut, so a discussion on some of the complications and concerns with euthanasia begin later in this chapter.

We must first consider this issue from a utilitarian standpoint by asking ourselves what legalized euthanasia would do to our society. Can we assure that this practice will be used for its intended purpose? And, first and foremost, what precisely is its intended purpose? What do we hope to accomplish through the practice of euthanasia? These are all-important questions, and ones that cannot easily be answered. It would seem that our goal with euthanasia is to assure the people involved a "good death," freeing them from further pain and hardship. This seems, on the surface, to be a perfectly understandable goal. Yet it is nearly impossible to assure someone a "good death." We can give them comfort and support, but in the end their acceptance of death rests largely on the way they lived their life. If they have led a full and satisfying life, an easy and peaceful death may be the perfect end.

However, if one has not led a fully satisfying life, they may use death as an escape, rather than a proper end. The type of euthanasia described here is known as voluntary, where the patient chooses to end his or her life. However, there are cases where the patient is unable to choose when his or her life should end. In these cases, a third party, be it a doctor, spouse, or family member, must step in and decide what it best for the patient, though this intervention would only complicate the situation further. Even someone close to the patient cannot always accurately determine what the patient would want. Emotional and personal ties to the patient also influence the ability of a person to make this decision. If a family member or spouse does not step in, some suggest a doctor should have the authority to end the patient's life. While a doctor possesses the medical expertise necessary for diagnosing and treating the patient, it is unlikely that he or she has received the proper training needed to make such a monumental decision. This type of euthanasia is known as non-voluntary. The final form of euthanasia is involuntary, where euthanasia takes place against the patient's wishes. While in certain cases, voluntary and non-voluntary euthanasia are allowed, involuntary euthanasia is not legal in any form.

Before we proceed further, it is important to distinguish between active and passive euthanasia. Passive euthanasia occurs when the medical treatment needed to sustain life is withheld from the patient. This includes anything from major surgery to refusing the patient food and water. Active euthanasia takes place when someone, be it the patient or a third party, takes an active means to end the patient's life, including lethal injection or intentional overdose. Active euthanasia can be further divided into two categories: assisted and non-assisted. If the euthanasia is voluntary, it is equivalent to suicide for the patient; in almost all cases of assisted euthanasia, it is equivalent to murder for the assistant.

While it may seem easy to distinguish active and passive euthanasia, there is a very fine line between killing a patient and letting a patient die. Passive euthanasia, some argue, is simply letting nature take its course. However, if the patient were living naturally, he or she would have the basic sustenance needed for life, such as food and water. This argument does prove effective in the cases where a patient refuses major surgery or artificial means to stay alive. In the case of active, non-assisted euthanasia, complications arise when one considers the mental stability or situation of the patient. A patient with a terminal illness may become extremely depressed, and, with the addition of various drugs, may be unable to make clear and reasonable decisions. An outside party might also create a situation in which they do not kill the patient themselves, but, with knowledge of the patient's mental state, provide the means and opportunity for the patient to take his or her own life. Does this, then, cross over into the realm of assisted euthanasia? This is simply another ill-fitting piece of the puzzle. Assisted euthanasia is, perhaps, the most confusing of the three types. Even if euthanasia is voluntary on the part of the patient, the assistant may have encouraged or influenced their decision to end their life. When considering non-voluntary euthanasia, the question becomes, What constitutes murder? The life of the patient is ending without their consent and without knowledge of their will. Involuntary euthanasia is almost always viewed as murder; it is the taking of a life against the known wishes of the patient.

The purpose of euthanasia is often said to be associated with compassion: a desire to eliminate pointless suffering and assure one's optimum comfort and peace. However, the main problem in this suggestion lies within the use of the arbitrary term "pointless." It is difficult to determine when suffering is pointless and when, if ever, it is necessary. Suffering to overcome an illness or problem would seem necessary, while suffering in the face of a terminal disorder might seem pointless. However, here we must distinguish between what we believe is pointless and what is pointless in the overall scheme of things. Many religious thinkers argue that there is a higher power with a specific plan for us all, and that humans should not intervene in matters of life and death. It is likely they would not view any suffering as pointless; they would likely decide that it has some purpose, even if it is one we ourselves cannot determine.

A major concern for many when dealing with euthanasia is the sanctity of life. Life, many believe, is a gift from a higher power, and is not to be tampered with by humans. Even so, sanctity of life might also mean dignity in death. If all life is sacred, is it right to allow it to continue when one is barely living and can no longer enjoy or take part in the life they have been given? A peaceful and easy death, chosen by a patient, may be a more fitting end to a life than one where the patient is in pain and uneasy with their death.

The compassionate side of euthanasia might seem, on the surface, to be utilitarian. However, ending the suffering of a single person would not likely affect the overall happiness of society. The concern here is the suffering of one person, without regard to effect on the community as a whole.

In contrast to the thinkers mentioned in the previous paragraph, there are those who argue that there is a right to die. They differ from those who respect the sanctity of life in one important way: they view life as property rather than a gift. They do not see it as the will of a higher power; rather, they see it more as an accident that entitles the individual to full possession of it. Therefore, they argue that the ability to decide to end one's own life is a right and not a privilege.

The problems with euthanasia include both the moral and legal. There are questions of who is qualified to make the decision to end life, what constitutes murder, and when suffering is truly unnecessary. Only when these questions are fully resolved can we make the decision of whether or not to legalize euthanasia.

Questions:
1) What should be done when passive euthanasia doesn't get the job done? When does assistance become necessary?

2) What criterion should be met in order for the suffering to be great enough to utilize euthanasia?

3) If euthanasia is considered acceptable, what restrictions should be put on it? How can a slippery slope be prevented?

4) Do you think that allowing euthanasia decreases the respect for life?

5) Would the legalization of euthanasia encourage discrimination against old people? Would older people then be pressured into euthanasia against their wishes?

6) What do you consider a "good death"?

Capital Punishment: The Case of Tom

Tom is a seventy-year-old death row inmate. He has been in prison for 52 years. When he was eighteen years old, he was convicted for the double murder of two African-American men. Because he was eighteen at the time of the murders, he was tried as an adult and received the death penalty.

Born and raised in a racist southern family, Tom was brought up in an environment where white supremacists were prevalent. His father,

84

grandfather, and uncles were all active members of the Ku Klux Klan and, from day one, Tom was taught to hate blacks. Influenced by these relatives, Tom soon joined the family tradition and became a part of the Klan.

When he was eighteen, however, he was caught and convicted for the murders of two young black men. He was sentenced to death, but because of loopholes in the system and repeated appeals, he has been kept alive in prison for almost all of his life. During his time in prison, Tom became a Christian and realized how wrong his previous lifestyle had been. Although a changed man, the time has now come for Tom's execution, and Tom has decided one last time to try for an appeal.

Another appeal for a death sentence would cost the state hundreds of thousands of dollars. If the death penalty is dropped, Tom will spend the rest of his life in prison and free up state funds that could be used elsewhere. That decision, however, could lessen any deterrent effect of the criminal justice system.

➤ What should the state do?

Framing the Issue: Punishment and the Death Penalty

Crime and punishment. Since the beginning of human civilization, society has been forced to deal with those who fail to abide by the laws of their community, deciding what constitutes a crime, who deserves punishment, and what that punishment should be. Throughout all these questions, one principle remains clear: punishment must be deserved. To force punishment on someone who has not committed a crime is clearly unlawful. What is not so clear is how the punishment of the perpetrator should relate to their crime. Should it be "eye for an eye"? Should it be designed to improve future situations? And most importantly, What is the goal of punishment?

To answer this question, we must understand the ways in which punishment can be viewed. These ways fall under the categories of backward-looking justifications and forward-looking justifications. Backward-looking justifications view punishment as retribution for a crime, as a way of equalizing the situation. Forward-looking justifications, however, see punishment as a way of affecting future situations. These justifications can be broken down into the deterrence model and the rehabilitative model. The deterrence model states that the goal of these justifications is to deter the perpetrator and others from committing the same crime, while the rehabilitative model deals more with rehabilitating and helping the criminal to overcome their problem with the hope that this will prevent them from committing the offense again.

Backward-looking justifications can also be seen as retributivism, or the idea that punishment is retribution for a past crime. Retributivism supports an "eye for an eye" philosophy (also known as lex talionis) in which a certain crime entails equal punishment. Critics of retributivism argue that it is simply a thinly veiled form of revenge, a primitive instinct disguised as a moral action. Advocates of retributivism respond to this argument in two ways. They may embrace the idea of retributivism as revenge and then argue that revenge is not an unreasonable impulse and is, in fact, a healthy and normal response to wrongdoing. Or they may choose to argue that retributivism is not revenge but instead balances the scales of justice by assuring that the perpetrator receives what he or she deserves. It is about equalizing the situation and giving equal punishment for equal actions, thus focusing on balancing justice because of larger ethical concerns. Others, however, choose to focus on the rights of the victims, arguing that a victim has a right to see the criminal suffer equally for his or her crime. Clearly, if the victim took the punishment of the perpetrator into his or her hands, the result would be anarchy, so it is reasonable that the state should assure that the victim's rights are respected. Yet another view of retributivism focuses on the effect of punishment on the perpetrators, arguing that punishment will bring insight or that criminals must experience the pain they have inflicted on their victims. Some also claim that punishment is a way for criminals to redeem themselves: by suffering for their crimes, they have repented and are ready to re-enter society and the moral community.

There are, however, several problems with the idea of retributivism. The main problem lies in the justification of punishment. Retributivists indicate that punishment is necessary because it is right, rarely offering another reason for its institution. The basis of retributivism, or the "eye for an eye" philosophy, also does not hold up well in the view of critics. If we take these words to heart, how do we determine the proper punishment for someone who has committed rape? How do we determine punishment for other, less defined crimes, such as plagiarizing a term paper? These questions seem to indicate that the phrase lex talionis cannot be taken literally.

Another idea of punishment, the deterrence model, is best viewed from a utilitarian viewpoint. By deterring the criminal and others from committing the offense, we are reducing the overall crime rate and, therefore, improving society as a whole. With this idea we are, of course, assuming that punishment reduces crime. In general, this assumption proves to be true. However, there is some question about how certain punishments affect the criminal and others who might be tempted to commit the crime. The question of whether punishment is the best way of reducing crime also presents itself. There are other possible ways to accomplish this goal: social programs, such as welfare and strong moral education, or through strong family and community support. These means of reducing crimes intend to be preventative, while punishment is largely a retrospective action.

Another assumption of the deterrence model is that reducing crime is necessarily good, given that one may object to certain measures of crime control that conflict with the rights and liberties of individuals. There is also a concern over whether disproportionate punishments will be given to the perpetrators of certain crimes, simply to deter others from committing the crime. The deterrence model seems to indicate that if it serves to reduce crime, any punishment is morally acceptable, even if it is not equivalent to the crime committed. To take this idea to the extreme, it would appear that punishing the innocent is acceptable if it accomplishes the goal of deterring crime. Punishing someone who the public thought was guilty would most likely produce a deterrent effect, even if the person had not actually committed the crime. This, again, infringes on the civil liberties of an individual.

The final view of punishment discussed in this chapter is the rehabilitation model. This idea perceives the criminal not as someone evil who has chosen to do wrong, but as someone in need of help who was largely a victim of circumstance. Our current prisons do not seem to accomplish this goal: they simply seem to strengthen criminals and provide them with new information and ideas for committing further crimes. However, rehabilitation programs would be difficult to create and establish. It would be difficult to determine what would help the perpetrator, how long they would need to be in such a program, and what the structure of this program would be.

There is perhaps no legal penalty in the American judicial system as controversial as capital punishment. For many, this punishment is unsettling because of the finality and irrevocability of death. There is no chance for reform of the criminal, though there is a possible deterrence effect for others. In the debate over capital punishment, we again encounter the idea of lex talionis, viewing the death penalty as "a life for a life." We can avoid some of the questions raised by the literal interpretation of lex talionis by viewing it as a law of proportionality: we give our harshest punishments for our worst crimes. However, this view raises different questions. Why are rape and torture not used as means of punishment? What really makes one punishment worse than another? In terms of cruelty, rape and torture can be viewed as worse than even the death penalty, since capital punishment is often accomplished by relatively painless means. However, one can recover from rape and torture, and may even succeed in reentering society and beginning a new life. Execution, however, cuts off all possibilities for a new beginning. It allows no chance for recovery or a new life. In this sense, death is the worst punishment. Since the point of punishment in our society, however, is not primarily to inflict pain, the death penalty seems more acceptable than the aforementioned punishments.

We encountered the issue of the sanctity of life in our discussion of euthanasia, an idea that is also relevant when dealing with death penalty. Here we can distinguish between the three separate views on the sanctity of life: the strong version, the moderate version, and the weak version. The strong version argues that the taking of a human life is immoral under any circumstances. Naturally, advocates of this version would oppose the death penalty. The moderate version opposes the taking of any innocent human life, indicating that its only opposition to the death penalty is the fact that innocent people might mistakenly be executed. The weak version states only that there must be an extremely strong justification for the taking of another human life. However, advocates of this version also argue that the death penalty should not be used because its justifications are not strong enough to constitute its use instead of life imprisonment.

Since capital punishment is irrevocable and final, many are concerned about innocent people who would receive this punishment. The American judicial system is not infallible; it has, in fact, been calculated that since 1900, fifty-seven people whose innocence can now be proven were executed. This does not, of course, take into account those who were innocent but have not yet been proven to be. Those who oppose the taking of any innocent human life would argue that this invalidates the death penalty. However, utilitarian thinkers would likely compare the number of innocent lives lost through execution to the innocent lives saved by the deterrence and elimination of criminals.

Capital punishment is a difficult issue to resolve because, like many other issues, it involves matters of life and death. We are, as a society, taking someone's life into our hands, and deciding when and why it should end. The death penalty can be seen as a last resort. We must decide if we, as a moral community, are prepared to face the responsibility of allowing our government to decide matters of life and death and if we believe capital punishment is truly the most appropriate penalty for our worst crimes.

Questions:
1) Should society concentrate more on retribution or deterrence?

2) Is it okay to give up certain civil liberties (such as privacy) in order to reduce criminal activities?

3) Is the "eye for an eye" method a just punishment? Is it always applicable? What should be done in situations where it is not appropriate?

4) Are there other ways to deter crime besides punishment?

Diversity: The Case of College Admissions

At Lincoln State University (LSU) in Illinois, the new dean and Board of Trustees passed a new admissions policy for the school's scholarship program. The new policy stated that LSU would seek to admit qualified students who will provide an ethnically and racially diverse environment. At the time, the student body at LSU was 60% Caucasian, 30% African American, 5% Hispanic, and 5% other. Furthermore, 55% of the population was male while 45% was female.

Presently, LSU Office of Admissions is faced with a dilemma. They have received four applications for a four-year, publicly-funded scholarship. The committee has to select only one of the following students for the scholarship.

Thadyeus Smith, a black male from inner city Detroit, is an "A" student at a public high school. His family is of low income. His father is only a high school graduate and his mother a housewife. Thadyeus was the president of his senior class and scored a 1050 on the SAT.

Jose Rodriguez, a Hispanic male from inner city LA attended a private school with the help of financial aid where he made straight "B's." His family is of lower to middle income. His father is a medical technician at a local hospital in LA, and his mother is a librarian. Jose scored a 1020 on the SAT.

From the suburbs of Baltimore, Janet Moore, a black female, is a "B" student at a public school. She comes from an upper income family, her father is a doctor and her mother is a high school teacher. Janet scored a 1260 on the SAT.

Paul Sampsonite is a white male from rural Illinois. He is a straight "A" student and Class Valedictorian. His family is of middle income. His father is a postal worker and his mother is a retail salesclerk. Paul's score on the SAT was a 1320.

➢ Which candidate should the board choose and why. Remember the policy at the beginning of the case.

Framing the Issue: Race and Ethnicity

We are Americans. We are all living together in a unique and advanced nation: a nation that is not made up of only one race or ethnicity, but a country that is a combination of cultures, backgrounds, and beliefs; hence, race is not the primary basis of one's

93

identity as an American citizen. In this chapter, we must ask ourselves two important questions: What role does race play in our society, and how do we equalize the citizens of our society without devaluing different cultures?

The first ideas we must separate here are those of race and ethnicity. Race is, in scientific terms, a physical characteristic, while ethnicity commonly refers to someone's culture and background. Race and ethnicity are not that different, however, in that race is not just a physical characteristic, but often carries more cultural significance. From these initial distinctions, we can focus on what happens when these characteristics are used against the person who possesses them. Discrimination based on race is known as racism; however, there is no corresponding term for discrimination on the basis of ethnicity. Racism has been a prevalent problem in American society since the foundation of this nation, beginning with the mistreatment of Native Americans by early settlers. America struggled with slavery, the mistreatment of Japanese-Americans, and discrimination against immigrants. Though we have greatly reduced the racist feelings and ideals in our country, we have not yet eliminated them completely. Racism is a problem that we must deal with if we are to live and work together as one nation.

Before we proceed further, we must answer our first question: What role does race play in our society? There have been several ideas presented as answers to this question, the main three being the separatist model, the assimilation model, and the pluralistic

94

model. The separatist model presents race and ethnicity as the principal basis for one's identity as a person, both as a form of discrimination against ethnic minorities and because some ethnic groups themselves favor separatism as a way of preserving their culture. Many Native-Americans, for example, have embraced the idea of separatism because it provides them with a way to continue their way of life without intrusions from outsiders. Other groups, such as the Amish and the Mennonites, advocate separatism on religious grounds. In larger cities, many groups congregate in neighborhoods based on their ethnic background, where they can speak their own language and practice the customs of their culture. Critics of this model point out that it divides the American community as a whole, and does not encourage different groups to learn about or interact with different cultures.

The assimilation model focuses largely on equalizing the American citizens through breaking down differences in culture and race until we have created a nation of individuals who are largely the same in culture and ideas. This model is often associated with the "melting pot" idea of American society, where all cultures are melted together until they have formed an overall American culture, with no smaller divisions. While this is effective as a means of equalizing our society, it ignores the importance of background and culture to many Americans. The final model is known as the pluralistic model, which realizes that diversity is important, but that we all must learn to function in a larger community. Diversity allows different ideas to thrive in our community. Without this variety of thought, we would create a stagnant intellectual, moral, and political community.

Another important question when dealing with racism concerns deciding who is responsible for past and present racism and how they should seek to amend their actions. We must recognize that there is a difference between government-sanctioned racism and racism that is not endorsed by any government institution. The purpose of a government is largely to carry out the wishes of citizens. Therefore, there is a question of whether the citizens under a racist government are responsible for the actions of that government. In the case of racism carried out by individuals or other unofficial groups, we must decide if we are responsible for correcting their attitudes and actions. After all this has been defined, we are then left with the responsibility of deciding what should be done about racism. Can we correct past wrongs, or can we only focus on improving the future? Those who believe racism should be viewed from a backwards-looking standpoint often advocate compensatory programs. They believe that because our government carried out acts influenced by racism, it is our responsibility as citizens to ensure that those who were wronged by our government are properly compensated. This, therefore, excludes us from compensating those who were discriminated by individuals, because they were not acting in our name. These compensatory programs also require us to help groups who were discriminated against regardless of their current economic state. Even if they have achieved economic success despite discrimination, backward-looking programs focus only on past wrongs and not current situations. These programs are also largely morally symbolic; they acknowledge to those that have been wronged that we recognize that we have caused their hardship and that we are willing to rectify it.

The other approaches we will focus on are largely forward-looking. These include the equal rights approaches, the affirmative action approaches, and the special protection approaches. Equal rights approaches do not necessarily advocate active means to ensure equality for previously discriminated groups; they simply advocate the principal of equality for all groups, with no special consideration for different divisions. Affirmative action programs however, generally support active means to secure equal rights and opportunities for minority groups. There are two meanings to affirmative action. The weak sense suggests two possible ways of correcting racism: encouraging the largest number of minority candidates to apply for a certain position and then choosing a candidate regardless of minority difference, or, when there are two equally qualified candidates for a job, choosing the minority candidate over the non-minority one. The strong sense of affirmative action suggests slightly more intensive means: when there is a pool of qualified applicants, choosing a minority applicant over more qualified non-minority ones, or, in more extreme cases, choosing an unqualified minority candidate over a qualified non-minority one. While these policies seek to help those who may be at a disadvantage because of past discrimination, they also run the risk of being seen as encouraging a different kind of discrimination: reverse racism.

There is a question of when and where affirmative action programs are needed, and before such programs are implemented, we must answer these questions. Special protection approaches do not usually support such active means, but instead promote programs that protect the rights and identities of minorities. Two such programs include the prevention of interracial adoption and hate speech. Many groups, especially African-Americans, oppose interracial adoption because they argue that it deprives minority children of a strong racial and ethnic identity. Placing minority children with non-minority parents, they say, does not allow them to fully understand and experience their culture, thereby preventing the culture from thriving and being passed on. Another example of a special protection program is the effort to eliminate hate speech, the use of degrading language or actions towards another race or culture as a result of a prejudicial attitude. Many argue that hate speech is highly damaging to minority groups and that the government should prevent such slander. However, few reforms have been made in this area for several reasons. Government measures against hate speech would oppose one of the most basic dictums of the American constitution: free speech. Even if it is potentially harmful, the right to speak freely is one of America's unique and treasured rights. It is also difficult to determine just what constitutes hate speech. If the government were given the ability to control hate speech, how would they decide what to allow and what to prevent?

There is no question that if we want to live in a successful and free society, we must ensure that all citizens are treated equally and that racism is eliminated. The question that remains for us, then, is how we should seek to create the sort of community in which people of all races, background, and beliefs, can live together with respect and equality.

Questions:
1) Should the government compensate oppressed groups, even though those who were originally wronged are now dead? Why or why not?

2) Why would some groups find separatism a good idea? What about assimilation? What are the pros and cons of each choice? Which do you think is better?

3) Do you consider affirmative action the right way to go about compensating minority groups? Why or why not? What other options are there?

4) Does affirmative action promote reverse discrimination? Are white males now becoming a discriminated-against class?

Sexual Harassment: The Case of Tiffany

Tiffany is a twenty-seven-year-old female who had had many different jobs throughout the years. She has spent most of her adult life working the system and has filed several lawsuits, including claims of sexual harassment.

After she lost her job as a waitress, she decides to interview at a local Garage and Auto Shop. When she goes for the interview, she learns that the job description entails making deliveries to the local garages within the area. Mike, the owner of the Shop, is hesitant to offer Tiffany the job because of the rough and almost entirely male environment that she would be working in. He voices this concern to Tiffany, who quickly assures him that she could handle it, and that she really wants the job. Mike decides that since having a female employee would help add to the company's image as well as fill the driver position, he would give Tiffany the job.

Tiffany begins working at the garage and quickly proves to her co-workers that while she is not a particularly hard worker, she does get the job done. A few weeks into the job, however, Tiffany comes to Mike with a complaint that one of the men made a crude comment to her. Mike confronts the employee and learns that the crude comment was actually just the employee's suggestion that Tiffany should meet him at a local bar later on that night. Mike asks the employee to watch his language and assumes that the matter is settled.

A few months later, Mike is shocked to find that Tiffany has filed a sexual harassment suit against another one of his employee's for what she calls discriminatory language. Tiffany claims that the employees giving her nicknames such as honey, doll, and babe are offensive to her. After an investigation into Tiffany's past, Mike realizes that this is not her first or even second time filing for sexual harassment, and she has made her living as a con.

Mike is afraid that if he continues to keep Tiffany under his employment, she will only cause problems in the workplace and might even file more claims of sexual harassment. If he fires her, however, chances are that she will claim that she was discriminated against because of her gender and take him to court. Mike is stuck; either decision could quite possibly cause him to end up in a lawsuit.

> What should Mike do and why? Should there be more restrictions on what sexual harassment really is?

Framing the Issue: Gender

Discrimination is one of the major factors that divides our society. It is what prevents us from uniting and moving forward as a nation, and it only fosters ignorance and hatred in our community. In the last section, we explored the problems posed by discrimination on the basis of race. We now turn to a different form of discrimination: that which is based on gender. Sexism is not a novel problem in American society; like racism, our government has, in the past, endorsed discrimination on the basis of gender. Men have rarely been affected by such discrimination, but women have suffered from government-sanctioned sexism since the foundation of our nation. Although the American government has largely eliminated sexist policies, sexism is still a major issue for our community today.

So what is sexism? What characterizes sexist attitudes and actions? The principal examples of sexism are sexist language, sex discrimination, sexual harassment, and rape. Sexist language is prevalent in our society and reflects how gender has commonly been viewed in our nation. Our language often forces us to identify a general person as male or female, regardless of their actual gender. We almost always revert to the pronoun "he" because we are unable to choose a gender-neutral pronoun. Some choose simply to say "he or she" or to change to plural pronouns for the purpose of neutrality. However, most of us still use "he" without a thought to the implications of its use. The second area of sexist language has to do with the discussion of sexual intercourse. Slang for sexual intercourse tends to be crude terms implying harm (such as screw). It is also common for women to be placed as the direct object of such sentences. This view presents women as sex objects and devalues them as partners.

The second division of sexism is known as sex discrimination. This includes overt job discrimination, comparable worth, and the theory and implantation of legal protection. When a woman is denied a job or promotion only because she is a woman, it is known as overt job discrimination. Although this form of discrimination has become far less prevalent in recent years, women are still paid less on the dollar than men, though how much of this difference is due to other factors (e.g., overtime, seniority, etc.) must be carefully distinguished from discriminatory practices.

There is also the issue of comparable worth, where professions that are predominantly female are paid less than occupations that are largely male. However, it is sometimes difficult to determine how to equalize the salaries of different positions and identify when gender discrimination actually plays a role in the differences in pay. The difficulties with the theory and implantation of legal protection are in the transition from the idea of equality of the sexes to ensuring its reality. Advocates of gender equality are worried that the government might claim to support such policies, but that they would not take adequate measures to ensure that these policies are carried out.

Women also face another problem: rape. While men may have to deal with homosexual rape in prison, they rarely encounter this concern in their daily lives. However, women are preyed upon more commonly and easily. Violence against women is also encouraged through media images and pornography. Pornography is a major concern for feminists because of the way it debases and devalues women. However, pornography technically falls under the category of free speech, and is thereby difficult to eliminate. Feminists also see reproductive rights as highly important to women. The right to choose whether or not to have children, they argue, gives women control of their body and prevents men from exploiting females' ability to reproduce.

Our society has struggled with this issue and has found no clear answer. There have, however, been several models created to answer the question of what the role of gender plays in our society. The first of these is known as the traditional model, which views the place of the woman as primarily in the home and the place of the man as primarily in the workplace. If women do choose to work, traditionalists argue that women should only occupy low-paying, menial, subservient, or child-related jobs. Traditionalists often defend this model by claiming that it creates a stable family environment. However, critics argue that this model forces women to be inferior both in the home and the workplace. They become less of an equal spouse and more of a maid or babysitter. Their work in the home is unpaid and their jobs in the workplace are underpaid. In an age where divorce is more accepted than it was some years ago, there is also danger in a woman becoming too dependent on her husband for financial support. Because of her lack of experience in the workplace, it would most likely be extremely difficult for her to find a sufficient job. The traditional model also places extra stress on the man, who must be the sole financial supporter of the family.

The second model we will examine in this chapter is known as the androgynous model. Advocates of this model say that gender should be as irrelevant in day to day life as eye color currently is. They argue that gender should not be considered in job selection, job salary, childcare, or any other rights. There are different opinions on how far the domain of the androgynous should actually stretch. Supporters of the androgynous model usually choose one of two levels of androgyny: weak androgyny or strong androgyny. Advocates of strong androgyny, the more extreme position, argue that gender-based distinctions should be completely eliminated in all possible areas of life.

However, some choose a milder version of this model, weak androgyny, which maintains that gender-based distinctions should not be permitted in public life, but are admissible in private and personal relationships. Critics of this model object to androgyny for several reasons. They often argue that androgyny is, quite simply, impossible. They claim that there are far too many differences between men and women for gender-based distinctions to be thrown aside completely. Others argue that while androgyny may be possible, it is not necessarily the goal we should be striving for. Critics of the androgynous model often use some of the same arguments used by critics of the assimilation model: namely, that androgyny would eliminate the diversity needed for a productive and understanding society. They say that the differences between men and women do not necessarily make one weaker than the other, but instead help them to create a diverse and intellectually stimulating community. These differences should be nurtured instead of ignored. It is probable, then, that they would advocate the third model, known as the maximal choice model. This idea does not seek to create a unisex society;

instead, it emphasizes free choice, saying that each individual should be allowed to choose what role gender plays in their lives. Gender-based distinctions should be eliminated from public life, and individuals should be free to choose what role it plays in their personal lives. Naturally, both traditionalists and supporters of the androgynous model object to this idea, though for different reasons.

Traditionalists claim that the lack of defined roles in the community would create confusion for society. Supporters of androgyny argue that the maximal choice model would simply be an illusion, and, due to social pressure, individuals would simply settle into the roles the majority chooses for them. They maintain that a more revolutionary step is needed to truly change society.

It is clear that before we pass any legislation with regard to gender, we must decide, as a nation, what role we want gender to play in our lives: whether something we can disregard or something we should use to determine our role in society.

Questions:
1) What should be done about unintentional sexism? Should it be punished? Why or why not? If so, to what extent?

2) How can we fix gendered language? Is it necessarily an offensive thing?

3) What can be done to make job availability and pay more equal between men and women?

4) What is considered sexual harassment? Should a woman's perspective be taken into account when harassment charges are brought up?

5) Should there be specific roles for men and women in the family? Why or why not?

6) What can be done about gender discrimination in all aspects of society?

Homosexuality: The Case of Mel

Mel is a 45-year-old husband and father of three. He is a conservative Christian, a seminary professor, and a church pastor. He and his wife Mary have been married for a little over twenty years, and their three children are teenagers or pre-teens. Mel has always been a leader in his church and the community. He seems to be a model husband and father.

For almost twenty-five years, Mel has been fighting his sexual orientation. His homosexual tendencies began in college. He fought these urges, however, because all of his life, Mel's church and parents taught that homosexuality is wrong, emphasizing key verses in Leviticus and Romans. So, for twenty-five years he went through every possible step to keep himself from becoming gay. He tried electroshock therapy, exorcism, and psychotherapy. He also kept all of these treatments a secret from his family.

After all the trauma and heartache he had struggled through, Mel finally realized that he had to face his true sexuality. He was gay, and there was no way he could hide it anymore. The first step he took was talking to his wife. Mary was in complete shock and they did not know what to do. He explained to her that he loved her and she had been a wonderful wife for over twenty years, but he was struggling against his true identity. Although he had always been against divorce and had even counseled couples against divorce, he felt that he needed to be free from this heterosexual relationship.

Mel felt that he needed to come to grips with who he really was and not try to hide his sexuality anymore. He found gay Christian support groups to help him with this struggle. They taught him that God would love him, and it would still be possible for him to be a good Christian even if he was gay. Even if he could reconcile his homosexuality and Christianity, Mel would still have to struggle with the dilemma of whether or not to leave his wife and children.

Mel wants to do what is best for his family but feels he cannot hide his sexuality any longer.

> ➤ Should Mel get a divorce, or should he stay married for the sake of his wife and children?

Framing the Issue: Sexual Orientation

Homosexuality is one of the more volatile issues facing our society today. Some people dislike talking or even thinking about it, while others feel pressured to resolve issues surrounding homosexuality because of the way these issues affect their lives and their society. Unlike racism and sexism, homosexuality has not always been a prominent issue in America. This is mostly due to the fact that homosexuality was not always openly displayed and therefore did not need to be considered in day-to-day life like race and gender. Today, however, people are becoming more comfortable revealing their sexual orientation, and, as a result, we find ourselves facing new and controversial issues about this topic.

What we must first understand is what sort of discrimination gays and lesbians encounter in American society. Because sexual orientation is not as apparent as race or gender, they may face little or no discrimination in their daily lives. Homosexuals have never been denied the right to vote, hold certain jobs, or own land, as women and African-Americans have. However, this does not mean they have not suffered discrimination. The American government publicly discriminates against gays and lesbians, refusing to allow them to serve openly in the military or legally marry. Homosexuals often face discrimination in child-related areas and are frequently abused and mocked for their sexual orientation.

We will now discuss in depth two obvious areas in which homosexuals face discrimination: military service and marriage. While President Clinton did make an effort to lift the ban on gays in the military in 1992 by instigating a "don't ask, don't tell" policy, they are still not permitted to openly serve their country in the armed forces. Supporters of this ban argue that the presence of homosexuals in the military would affect unit cohesion and troop morale. Homosexuals are also not allowed to enter into legally recognized marriages. This prevents them from receiving the marriage benefits to which heterosexual couples are entitled.

The arguments presented against homosexuality and equal rights for homosexuals are divided into three main categories. These categories are known as the religious arguments, intrinsic arguments, and extrinsic arguments. Religious arguments tend to focus either on religious texts or the religious tradition as a whole. Textual arguments point out specific section of sacred texts (such as the Bible or Koran) that seem to condemn homosexuality. However, those who argue with the religious tradition in mind consider the religious community as a whole. They focus less on the condemnation of acts and dwell more on the idea of a gay lifestyle. The principal question for these thinkers is whether a gay lifestyle is truly compatible with the overall religious tradition. This is a principal consideration in religious arguments: Is homosexual orientation or only a gay lifestyle sinful? Some religious thinkers embrace the idea of "Love the sinner, hate the sin," proclaiming that if gays and lesbians practice celibacy, they are fully welcome in the church. However, most gays do not favor this idea, saying that to deny their sexual orientation through celibacy is to deny a primary facet of their identity.

The intrinsic argument states that there is something intrinsically immoral about homosexuality, presenting several reasons for this idea. One of the primary arguments is that homosexuality is "unnatural." This presents two questions: one, how is homosexuality unnatural, and two, does unnatural equal immoral? Homosexuality can be viewed as unnatural because it is not the sexual orientation of the majority. However, there is evidence that homosexuality may be genetic, therefore qualifying it as "natural." After we discover the ambiguity in this issue, we must face the second question: does being unnatural immediately qualify something as being wrong? Disease and death, it could be argued, are "natural," but does this mean they are good? On the other hand, new life-saving medical procedures and medicines may be "unnatural," but does that qualify them as immoral? We soon find that it is impossible to determine what is meant by "natural" and "unnatural" and if these terms have any real significance. The final set of arguments is known as the extrinsic arguments. These focus less on homosexuality itself and more on the factors associated with homosexuality. Advocates of extrinsic arguments often argue that homosexuals have less permanent and more promiscuous relationships than heterosexuals, and so it is immoral to encourage them. However, because of society's still-biased view of homosexuality, it is hard to determine if this argument is true. Secondly, one must take into consideration that those involved in homosexual relationships do not always have the support of their friends, family, and community the way heterosexual

111

couples do. This may make it difficult for a couple to form a permanent relationship.

As with race and gender, we must now decide where sexual orientation fits into our society. However, here we face another level we did not encounter in our previous discussions: the question of whether homosexuality itself is moral. This was not an issue in race or gender; however, it is an extremely important consideration in this discussion. There are three primary models presented for the role of sexual orientation in our society: the traditional model, the liberal model, and the polymorphous model. The traditional model, usually supported by conservatives, allows no place for homosexuality in society. Being homosexual would either eliminate someone from the community, or, one would have to pledge celibacy in order to remain within society. Advocates of this argument offer a few main reasons for their support: one, that homosexuality is intrinsically immoral and therefore should not be tolerated, and two, that homosexuality contradicts the basic values of society (such as the emphasis on family life). Critics point out that the intrinsic argument has already been proven to be highly unclear and is therefore irrelevant. They also refute the values argument in one of two ways: either by arguing that the values of society should be encouraged, but are not the required values of every citizen in the community, or secondly, by arguing that many gays and lesbians support family life and would even like to adopt and raise children of their own. We find three different ideas of the role of sexual orientation within the liberal model. The first of these ideas is tolerance, which states that gays and lesbians should be allowed to live in society without discrimination, but should not be encouraged to pursue their lifestyle. Many supporters of this model may believe homosexuality is wrong but do not believe the government should regulate morality. We then move on to the idea of acceptance, which argues that homosexuals should be allowed to declare their sexual orientation openly just as heterosexuals do. This model also calls for the legal protection of gays and lesbians.

Finally, endorsement, the most extreme version, declares that homosexual lifestyles should be presented as a sound and moral alternative to a heterosexual lifestyle. This version might include legally sanctioning gay marriages, presenting gay and lesbian families in public school curricula, and encouraging homosexuals to adopt. The final model, known as the polymorphous model, sees sex as a tool for pleasure and not as a means for procreation or intimacy. Therefore, this argument allows for any sort of sexual act that brings pleasure, potentially opening the door for such practices as bestiality.

The positions regarding homosexuality differ so extremely that it may be difficult to come to some sort of consensus on the issue in the near future. However, we may be able to resolve some of the smaller issues associated with homosexuality before we take a stance on the overall topic.

Questions:
1) What types of discrimination are there against

homosexuals? Should there be laws protecting them from these discriminations?

2) What problems are caused by gays in the military? Can they be fixed? If so, should gays and lesbians be allowed to openly join the ranks?

3) Is the traditional religious distinction between homosexual orientation and homosexual lifestyle (condemning the sin but not the sinner) a helpful one?

4) Is the "natural" argument helpful? Does it really matter in the issue?

5) If homosexuality is hereditary, how might our viewpoints towards homosexuals change? How might it affect their positions in society and our attitudes towards them?

6) To what extent should society support the homosexual choice? Is that a realistic goal?

7) Is a common ground possible where values could agree with both homosexual and heterosexual viewpoints?

Homelessness: The Case of Harry

Harry is a harmless man who roams the streets of Minneapolis. His parents died in a car crash when he was nineteen, leaving him to get along on his own. He was married when he was twenty-five, but a year later his wife divorced him.

At present, Harry cannot keep a job, and he spends all of the little money he has on cigarettes and alcohol. Harry begs for money and digs through trashcans each day for food. He is mildly retarded and has a borderline personality disorder. When his wife was married to him, she thought that he was crazy and admitted him to a psychiatric hospital. He was not helped there and was harassed by his roommates. He was released from the psychiatric hospital because he did not want to live his life trapped in such a place and preferred just to roam the streets.

This is Harry's first year since his hospital discharge, and he has never experienced the biting cold of the winters in Minneapolis. Even though many would consider his life dreadful, he has found a place outside of the train station where he sleeps every night and stores the things he has collected from the trash.

One night while walking towards the train station, Harry comes across a homeless shelter. He is told that he should stay at the shelter and sleep in a warm bed because the temperature is predicted to be ten degrees below freezing for the night. Harry is afraid to go into one of these shelters because it reminds him of the awful tortures of being institutionalized. He is also afraid that if he does not go to his little dwelling, all of his treasures will be stolen. Because the man at the shelter feels sorry for Harry, he considers giving Harry some money in the hopes that he will use it to find another place to stay (one that Harry is more comfortable with) and a hot meal to eat. However, he also considers the fact that Harry may very well use the money to buy alcohol or drugs instead. The worker is torn: on the one hand, he could be helping this man get back on his feet; on the other, he could be leading Harry further into poverty and troubles.

> What should the man at the shelter do? Consider the long and short-term effects of giving money to the poor.

Framing the Issue: Poverty and World Hunger

The world is not a perfect place. We are constantly struggling with the issues of poverty and hunger, searching desperately for some solution to these problems. In this chapter, we will first examine poverty on a national level; we will then expand our discussion and include issues such as world hunger and poverty.

Perhaps the most important consideration when discussing poverty is why it occurs. Establishing this basis will allow us to determine if this is a problem we are obligated to solve, and if so, how we are to go about remedying it. There have been three main models presented to explain the origins and nature of poverty: the discrimination model, the random market forces model, and the just deserts model. Advocates of the discrimination model claim that poverty is a direct result of mainly racial, but also sexist, discrimination. They believe that past and present discrimination has resulted in the

116

impoverishment of a majority of families and individuals. However, critics often cite Jews, Irish, Italians, and Asians as groups that have managed to endure and overcome discrimination.

The random market forces model argues that poverty is not based on discrimination or individual merit, but is a result of the impersonal forces of the economic market. Jobs are created and lost, entire industries may rise and fall within a matter of years, and there is little that we can do about it.

Finally, the just deserts model of poverty asserts that poverty is simply the result of laziness or poor moral character. It claims that poverty is a form of retribution for a lack of motivation and moral character. Furthermore, it maintains that the government should not support these people because this only allows them to continue living without any pressing need to find a job or be productive. Even if impoverished people are found to be largely responsible for their current economic state, we must consider that many of these individuals have children. These children are innocent in the matter of their economic state; it was not their poor decisions or lack of motivation that brought them to poverty. The arguments for helping children are commonly presented in one of two ways. Some argue that compassion should be the primary basis for our assistance of children. We realize their suffering, sympathize with their pain, and strive to alleviate it. Others offer a more concrete reason for assuring children a better future. They focus on the circle of poverty--a dangerous cycle that often results in

117

children of impoverished parents growing up to be impoverished adults. Assuring these children the means to support themselves in the future will benefit society as a whole because it will reduce the rate of poverty. Therefore, the circle of poverty approach can be classified as utilitarian.

We now face another question: does our government have an obligation to help these people? What is the government's role in reducing poverty? There are three social, political philosophies that pertain not only to poverty, but also to other important issues in our daily lives. The self-regulating model is represented by libertarianism and conservatism, both of which believe that the government will function best if left alone. Advocates of this model claim that government intervention would only aggravate a poor economic situation. The opposite of this idea is the strong interventionist model, represented by the governmental models of communism and socialism. This model endorses the idea of strong government intervention in order to create a society in which all citizens are relatively economically equal. The final model, known as the moderate interventionist model, tries to establish more of a middle ground. Commonly supported by modern liberals, this model states that citizens would not be allowed to sink below a certain level, but would have no limits on how much wealth they could accumulate.

We are now responsible for deciding how we should approach poverty. Three different approaches, the rights-based approach, the consequentialist approach, and the compassion-based approach, have been presented to resolve this issue. Advocates of the rights-based approach tend to favor either the discrimination model or the random market forces model. They believe that poverty is simply a combination of discrimination and bad luck, and that it is, therefore, the government's responsibility to see that their right to an equal economic situation is upheld. Others favor the consequentialist approach to poverty, which does not consider whether an individual has the right to welfare, but only consider what the consequences of their support (or lack thereof) will be. Supporters of this view argue that creating welfare programs or other programs to reduce poverty will eventually benefit all of society, lending a utilitarian tint to their views. They claim these sorts of programs will eventually lead to a more capable workforce, a physically healthier population, and less crime due to overall increased economic prosperity. However, critics of this approach question the ability of these programs to produce the benefits this model promises. They further argue that such programs may lead to unwanted consequences, such as families becoming dependent on welfare. The children of such families, they claim, may rely on such welfare programs when they become adults. The final approach, known as the compassion-based approach, appeals to our basic moral instincts. They claim the issue is not about causes or rights; rather, it is based on a desire to reduce the suffering of others. Critics often argue that emotion, however well intentioned, may be misdirected or create a worse situation.

So far, we have looked at poverty from a national point of view: our government's responsibilities to its citizens. However, we are not an isolated nation. We are rapidly developing into a global society--one that relies on and works with countries all over the world. We now find ourselves facing a difficult question: are we obligated to assist other countries that face problems such as widespread hunger, poverty, or problems due to natural disasters? One of the arguments in favor of helping other countries is known as the argument from virtue. Similar to the compassion-based approach, this idea says we must rely on the compassion we feel in our decision to assist others. They also argue that it is sheer luck that we were born into a fairly affluent and functioning society. Therefore, it is our duty to help those who were not so lucky. Some critics find problems with this last statement, arguing that whether societies are rich or poor is not simply a matter of luck; it is the people and governments within the nation that determine its success. However, advocates of assisting other countries often refute this argument with the claim that affluent countries are in part responsible for these problems. The argument here is that our success was built on impoverishing other nations and that we, therefore, have an obligation to better their society. The strict utilitarian argument, which advocates the greatest good for the greatest number of people, requires us to reduce or equalize the gap between rich and poor countries. It is important, however, to realize that as with any utilitarian argument, especially this one, some may find their quality of life or affluence reduced in order that another's may be improved. The "greatest" good does not mean the maximum for an individual; rather, it refers to the best possible when dealing with the largest amount of people.

The basic rights argument claims that all people have a right to basic subsistence. It is important to make the distinction here between a negative right and a positive right. A negative right means that no one is allowed to interfere with a right; a positive right entails that one is entitled to the means and support to carry out that right. Advocates of the basic rights argument often portray this as a positive right. Finally, the Kantian argument states that we are morally required to act benevolently. However, this is known as an imperfect duty, one that is morally required but not necessarily obligatory for all situations. Therefore, we are required to help other countries but have no duty to reduce our standard of living just so that we equalize the overall situation.

On the other hand, there are those who believe we should not assist other countries. Advocates of this view often refer to the lifeboat metaphor, which portrays rich countries as lifeboats that poor countries are desperately trying to board. If allowed to board, some claim that the boat will become swamped and the entire boat will drown. It is thus suggested that the boat be preserved at best quality instead of lowering its standards by attempting to crowd it with the most number of passengers possible.

However, critics claim that this argument is misleading. Poor countries do not wish to board the boat of wealthy countries but simply wish to keep their own vessel afloat. Others favor the effectiveness argument, stating that our aid is not truly beneficial to other nations for a variety of reasons. These include factors often out of our control, such as the administration, local economy, and the local corruption, or may include unwanted consequences, such as dependency or eventual futility. If our assistance does not truly better the situation, we are not morally obligated to provide it.

Libertarians tend to argue against supporting other countries because of their belief that all rights, including the right to life, are negative rights. Others have no obligation to support these rights. Another view, known as the particularity argument, asserts that we should not place the needs of strangers above the needs of our own. We should support and help those we love and interact with, but have no obligation to complete strangers. The liberal state argument takes a similar, though broader, stance: we should concern ourselves first and foremost with the economic state of our own nation. We must improve the quality of life of our citizens instead of using money for foreign aid.

As you can see, there are many differing viewpoints on this issue, viewpoints that cannot always be easily combined. One thing, however, is clear: we are interacting more and more with different nations. The state of those countries will affect the state of our world. Our duty now is to envision what sort of world we are striving for and how we shall create it.

Questions:
1) What do you think makes the poor impoverished? What factors must be considered?

2) What role should the government take in the economy? What are the advantages and disadvantages of each model?

3) What should be done about children caught in the cycle of poverty?

4) Are rich nations morally obliged to help poor countries, or is it just the compassionate thing to do?

5) Does foreign aid really help in the long run or is it just a short-term solution? Should we be teaching them to better their economy or agricultural techniques as opposed to just sending them money?

6) What are the different ways to help poor countries? What do you consider the best overall?

7) Are we obliged to ignore our own suffering in light of a deeper suffering in another country?

8) To what extent should we respond to poverty as a whole? What compromises can you come up with?

Animal Research: The Case of the Cure

Recently, scientists have discovered a new drug that doctors and scientists alike hope to be a key element in a cure for cancer. If effective, this drug would stop the growth of cancerous cells and then begin to eliminate all traces of cancer in the bloodstream. Millions of lives could be saved and cancer could well be on its way to being eradicated. Unfortunately, this drug appears to be a long shot and the researchers are far from certain that the drug will work.

In order for the drug to be FDA (Food and Drug Administration) approved, however, the drug must be tested and proven harmless to the patient with no negative long-term side effects. While the drug can be made available to the public on an experimental basis by choice, waiting for tests and results of the drug effects on humans could take decades to prove that not only is the drug effective but also harmless.

Testing the drug on animals, however, would greatly speed up the testing process, provide ample data for researchers, and keep humans from having to risk detrimental side effects. Unfortunately, the only way to test this drug is to inject rabbits and small rodents with cancerous cells and then treat them with different dosage amounts of the drug. If this experiment succeeded, the process would then be tried on larger animals such as cats and dogs in order to see if the drug worked on larger mammals as well. Depending on how well the drug worked, many animals could suffer or die from the injected cancerous cells. Furthermore, even with the larger mammal testing, there is still the possibility that the drug would not work on humans.

If the drug proves to help cure cancer, it could save millions of human lives. If it fails, many animal lives will be lost.

> ➤ Should the drug be tested on animals? Is it okay to experiment with animals if there is a possibility of saving human lives?

Framing the Issue: Animals & the Environment

So far, our discussions have centered only on issues that directly affect humans—issues concerning the economic, social, and political states of our world. However, in this chapter we will focus less on the people living on earth and more on the earth itself. We will also consider the other inhabitants of this world, asking ourselves how far our moral concerns should extend. Do animals deserve equal moral treatment? And, if so, how will this change the way we live? Many of us consume animal products, such as meat, eggs, or dairy, and may wear leather or benefit from procedures and medicines previously tested on animals. We interact with animals on a fairly constant basis, whether it is through our pets and zoos or hunting and fishing. So how do we determine if they deserve the moral consideration we extend to humans?

An important consideration in this issue is religious concerns. Christian traditions tend to deny animals equal moral status for several reasons. They argue

125

that in Genesis, the first book of the Bible, animals are portrayed as existing solely for the sake of human beings. This gives them only an instrumental value, not an intrinsic one. Others claim that because Jesus is said to be the incarnation of God in human form, this places humans on a higher level than animals. Finally, many assert that while humans have an immortal soul, animals do not, thus allowing them no moral status.

However, some Christians do cite certain passages of Genesis as evidence of God's command to care for the earth. This does not necessarily mean that we should consider animals equal to humans, but that we should care for their environment and ensure their relative safety. Buddhists, on the other hand, advocate the equal treatment of animals for two reasons that are integral to their religious tradition. One of these aspects is the Buddhist belief of compassion and respect for all life, not just human life. All suffering should be regarded as equal. Buddhism also teaches reincarnation, the belief that souls move through different earth-bound forms on their search for enlightenment. Buddhism drastically differs from Christianity in the idea that animals have a soul. Finally, Native American religions emphasize a harmonious relationship with all things living, but do not usually prohibit or condemn animal killings. Instead, they stress the importance of respect for the animal and using all parts of its body for productive purposes.

After we have discussed the theological concerns, we should consider this issue from a utilitarian viewpoint. Within utilitarianism, we find a very important question: is the issue concerned only with the suffering and welfare of humans, or that of all living beings? The original form of utilitarianism, created by Jeremy Bentham, was far more sensitive towards animals than most other ethical traditions. However, some variations of this basic form concern themselves only with the well being of humans. If we look at this issue from this point of view, we find arguments in favor of animal rights. A diet rich in meat might be potentially harmful to the health of a human, and cruelty to animals might negatively affect their mental state. Although animal rights activists can use either of these two arguments, we still find ourselves confused as to the ultimate purpose of utilitarianism. This leaves us with a fundamental concern: Who has rights, and why? What do we consider necessary for a right to life? We may find ourselves facing some of the same issues we discussed in our debate on abortion: ability to feel pain, metacognition, and the presence of a soul. The question of why someone or something is entitled to rights is one of the basic issues we must resolve in order to take action on this topic.

As in several previous issues, we find that many use pure compassion as motivation for reducing the suffering of others. However, as we have found in previous discussions, this moral foundation can sometimes be ambiguous and misdirected. Some argue that compassion is not really an issue, since few of us actually kill the animals we consume. This lack of proximity may reduce our strong feelings of compassion for animals, somewhat like caring about strangers in countries other than our own. Critics, however, assert that ignorance is no excuse for a lack of caring and respect. We often choose not to think of where our meal or clothing items come from, purposefully ignoring the issue and refusing to face the feelings such thoughts may summon.

Let us now turn to the terms of our specific interactions with animals, which include medical experimentation, commercial animal agriculture and consumption, and pets. When faced with the decision of saving a human life or an animal's, most of us would choose the human. However, in medical experimentation, the terms are rarely that simple. We find ourselves faced with the decision of whether to save a human life at the cost of perhaps hundreds of animal lives. In addition, animals used in medical research are not always being used to better society or cure diseases; often, they are used only to test new products or train students and laboratory workers in certain techniques. An issue many of us deal with more closely is commercial animal agriculture and consumption. Animal rights activists often use the reality of an animal's life on a commercial farm to inspire compassion. Animals raised in this sort of captivity are often deprived of a natural way of life, finding themselves unable to perform basic functions such as nursing, grooming, and pecking. Their lives eventually end in slaughter, making this an even more painful and effective picture. Some claim that this image alone is reason enough to become vegetarian and allow animals many human rights. However, others search for a middle ground, saying that animals raised on commercial farms should be allowed to lead natural lifestyles with as little human interaction as possible and should be killed in a way that minimizes pain.

Moving on, few see owning pets as a deprivation of animal rights; rather, they contend that a pet-owner relationship is a loving bond, with no benefit other than each other's company and attention. Critics of this idea immediately pounce on the word "owner," declaring that the use of this word reveals what the relationship between human owner and animal pet really is. Humans see their pets as pieces of property: they pay money for them and hold them in an environment that they would not naturally inhabit. However, some maintain that animals are actually happiest in their interactions with humans and safer than they would be in the wild. Therefore, they take an expanded utilitarian view and include animals' well being in the issue.

We have discussed how we regard animals; now, we must decide how we view our relationship with our world. Does it exist only to support us, or are their special considerations we must take that do not directly concern our own welfare? We can begin with human-centered approaches, which view the environment in terms of the needs and concerns of human beings. There are several forms of human-centered approaches, including ethical egoism, group egoism, and utilitarianism. Ethical egoism maintains that the only motivation for any action is self-interest. Therefore, if preserving the environment helps or pleases you in some way, it is a valid action. Group egoists are less concerned with self and more concerned with the group with which one is most closely affiliated. These groups may be quite narrow, such as family or friends, or extremely broad, such as one's nation or those who share the same religious beliefs. The version of utilitarianism that we find in this group, naturally, is the one that focuses only on the good of human society.

However, expanded-circle approaches take a broader view of the subject. We find expanded utilitarianism, an ethical tradition that advocates the consideration of all sentient beings in determining the greatest amount of good possible, in this group. Biocentrism has a teleological premise, meaning that it advocates rights for all living beings (including plants) on the basis that they have some telos, or final goal. Therefore, we are morally obligated not to thwart their natural goal. Ecocentrism is the most extreme version of the three expanded-circle approaches, as it considers everything existing on the earth, be it animate or inanimate. There are two possible forms of this idea, known as individual ecocentrism and holistic ecocetrism. Individualistic ecocentrism considers every separate and specific entity in an ecosystem and assigns it a moral weight. Holistic ecocentrism, on the other hand, gives a moral weight to larger groups, such as certain species. We sometimes forget that we as a society are not the only beings who will be affected by our decisions and actions regarding the environment. Our children will inherit this earth, and we must decide how we will leave it for them. While debating this, we often face a philosophical conundrum: do our descendants have rights, despite the fact that they are non-existent beings? We expect that the human race has a future, and we must act accordingly.

Whose world is it? Who are we to decide? These are just a few of the most important questions we must consider in this debate. We must choose who has moral rights, what those moral rights are, and how they differ from species to species.

Questions:
1) Should pain be taken into consideration when regarding animal rights? How much weight should that pain carry and what is its relation to human pain?

2) What should be done about conflicting interests between species? Who or what has moral weight and how much?

3) How should animals be used in medical research and experiments?

4) What factors should be taken into account when deciding moral weight?

5) How does Christianity reflect both dominion and stewardship models towards animals?

ADDITIONAL CASE STUDIES

Abortion

The Case of Jim Sexton

Jim Sexton is a well-known, respected minister in a small town. He and his wife are family counselors. They have two daughters, ages seven and twelve.

One day the minister and his wife left their two daughters at home alone while they went shopping for the day in a nearby town. That day, a thief broke into the house and not only stole several valuables but also raped the two girls.

After about a month, the older daughter realized that she had missed a period and could be pregnant. The next week she went to the doctor, who confirmed her suspicions. The doctor suggested that she have an abortion. Because of her youth, going through labor and delivery could cause infertility or could possibly kill her, and the baby could suffer birth defects or even death. Additionally, carrying the pregnancy to term could cause psychological trauma in a twelve-year-old rape victim. Finally, she would be an outcast at school and unable to participate in the activities of a normal twelve-year-old.

She is not allowed to make her own decision because of her age; her decision is only acceptable with her parents' consent. She wants to do what the doctor thinks is best and wants to minimize the detrimental consequences, but she also wants her parents' support.

Jim and his wife have a reputation for opposing abortion and have routinely counseled older teenage girls who have engaged in consensual sex against it. This case, however, seems different: The girl is only twelve, she is a rape victim, and of course she is their daughter. If she did go through with the abortion, it could tarnish the Sextons' reputation as persons of character and as pro-life advocates.

➤ What should the family decide, and why?

The Case of Stephanie and Joe's Baby

Stephanie and Joe met while working at a local take-out pizza shop. They were both in college and found that they had many things in common. They began to date and eventually married. The newlyweds moved to another state when Joe matriculated into a graduate program in music. Stephanie worked full-time at a restaurant located near their home so that they could afford for Joe to go to school. They owned one car, so Stephanie dropped Joe at the bus stop before going into work every day. Finances were tight, but they made ends meet. They both wanted to have children, but the couple felt that it would be best to wait to have children until Joe was also able to help support the family.

Joe soon graduated with his master's degree and began to work at the university. Things were not as hard now since they both had jobs. When Stephanie became pregnant, they were excited that their dream to have children was now coming true.

They would be able to care for and love the children, and they would be able to financially support them as well. It was one of the happiest times in their lives. Stephanie received excellent prenatal care. She went in for regular check-ups and took good care of herself. Because she was a vegetarian, she made sure that she received all the vitamins that she and the baby would need during the pregnancy.

During one of the check-ups, an ultrasound indicated an abnormality. The baby had hydrocephalus, or water on the brain. Hydrocephalus occurs when one of the ventricles in the brain does not drain properly, and the skull begins to fill with fluid. In the baby's case, it was very deep in the brain. Normally, Stephanie and Joe would have only two possibilities: have an abortion or give birth to a retarded child. Their Christian convictions militated against abortion, so that was not an option.

Their physician mentioned another option. Dr. Spag, who specialized in intrauterine surgery, could insert a temporary shunt in the baby's brain that would drain the fluid into the baby's stomach. After the baby was born, he or she would go into immediate surgery to receive a permanent shunt. If done properly, brain damage would be less likely. Unfortunately, this was a new and relatively untested technique, so the baby could still die or have severe brain damage. Stephanie and Joe had to decide whether or not to risk the dangers of intrauterine surgery both to the baby and to Stephanie to give the baby an unknown chance at life.

➤ What should Stephanie and Joe do, and why?

Baseball

The Case of Mickey Mantle

Boy wonder Mickey Mantle was born on October 20, 1931, in Spavinaw, Oklahoma. During his childhood he was diagnosed with osteomyelitis, a bone disease that can cause crippling. The doctor told his family that his leg might have to be amputated; however, his disease was treated with penicillin and he recovered. He returned to play baseball and was signed by a New York Yankee scout in 1949. After spending only two seasons in the minor leagues, Mickey was then called up to play alongside the "Yankee Clipper," Joe DiMaggio, in right field. With the entire nation's eyes on Mickey Mantle's spectacular playing, he soon became an American hero and found himself caught up in a life of fame.

After his father died from cancer in 1949, Mantle turned to alcohol to soothe his loss. His drinking worsened, and there were even times that he played baseball with a hangover. Although he clearly had a drinking problem, he continued to perform on the field. In 1968, he retired from the game of baseball. No longer having the obligation to play, Mantle began drinking even more heavily.

In late May of 1995, doctors found a tumor of unknown malignancy in Mickey Mantle's liver. Although it is uncertain what caused the tumor, three possible contributing factors are known. Some doctors believe that Mantle's drinking problems were the sole reason for the tumor, while others believe that it was a combination of Mantle's Hepatitis C infection and alcohol. There is also a possibility that Mantle was more susceptible due to a family history of disease. His grandfather died at the age of forty from lymphatic cancer. His father died at the age of forty-one from Hodgkin's disease, and one of Mantle's brothers had been struggling with the same disease when he died at the age of thirty-six after a heart attack. Because of the severity of the cirrhosis, doctors claimed that Mantle would not survive without a transplant. Plus, a celebrity in need of an organ would likely increase donations from people wanting to help him. The mortality rate of the procedure, however, is twenty-five percent for someone this sick, whereas a healthy person's operative mortality rate is only five percent.

> Should a person who abuses his organs be able to receive an organ transplant?

> Is using a celebrity to publicize the need for donations ethical even if doctors believe the morbidity risk of the procedure is high?

> Should Mickey Mantle receive the liver over a less ill recipient?

The Case of Pete Rose

When one thinks of America's pastime, names such as Lou Gehrig, Joe DiMaggio, Jackie Robinson, and Hank Aaron come to mind as heroes of the game who achieved greatness by overcoming obstacles and acting with integrity and pride. Others such as

"Shoeless" Joe Jackson and Pete Rose excelled as baseball players, but they tarnished their reputations and sacrificed the game of baseball by gambling on baseball.

The Chicago White Sox of 1919, now well-known as the Chicago Black Sox, allegedly threw games in the 1919 World Series against the Cincinnati Reds. In 1919, there was no better team than the Chicago White Sox; however, they were both underpaid and poorly treated by their owner, Charles Comiskey. Some small-time gamblers offered bribes to players that were several times the players' salaries.

Although this had been occurring for over fifty years, no steps had been taken to deter players from taking bribes until accusations were brought against eight members of the 1919 Chicago White Sox team. Eddie Cicotte and Lefty Williams allegedly threw games of the 1919 World Series. "Shoeless" Joe Jackson, Eddie Cicotte, Lefty Williams, and five other players were all eventually charged with gambling on baseball, which resulted in a court trial. Although a lack of evidence resulted in a not guilty verdict, all eight were banned from baseball. The judge appointed by the commissioner of baseball stated, "Regardless of the verdict of the juries, no player who throws a ball game, no player who undertakes or promises to throw a ball game, no player who sits in confidence with a bunch of crooked players and does not promptly tell his club about it, will ever play professional baseball."

Similarly, Pete Rose, the Cincinnati Red known as "Charlie Hustle," was accused of engaging "in conduct not in the best interests of baseball in violation of Major League Rule 21, including but not limited to betting on Major League Baseball games in connection with which he had a duty to perform." Pete Rose, during his twenty-four Major League seasons, had a record-setting 4,256 career hits in a Major League record of 3,562 games played. Rose also had a .303 lifetime batting average and made history by being the only player to play in more than 500 Major League games at five different positions. Any one of these statistics would qualify Pete Rose for baseball's Hall of Fame were it not for his gambling addiction.

After he met several convicted felons involved in illegal gambling, drug dealing, and tax evasion, his gambling allegedly began and his life was quickly consumed by it. He bet on games during the 1985, '86, and '87 seasons, sometimes betting up to $30,000 a night. In order to gamble, he received loans from drug dealers in exchange for jewelry, cars, and even his 4,192nd hit ball and bat worth $129,000. There were even times when people showed up at spring training and in the clubhouse at Riverfront Stadium to collect his gambling debts. By this time, Pete Rose was distracted and overcome with gambling. In February 1989, the baseball commissioner's office began its investigation of Rose. The leading investigator, John Dowd, compiled a damaging case. Paul Janszen, one of Rose's creditors who was investigated by the FBI for drug dealing and tax evasion, finally began to cooperate with the FBI. With Rose owing Janszen thousands of dollars, Janszen told Dowd everything in exchange for only a six-month sentence. He confirmed that

Rose had indeed bet on baseball games and provided Rose's actual betting sheets.

In May 1989, Dowd's report was given to Commissioner Giamatti. On August 23, 1989, Rose accepted a lifetime suspension from baseball with the opportunity to apply for reinstatement in one year. In April 1990, he pleaded guilty for failure to report $348,720 on his income tax report and was sentenced to five months in prison. In November 1999, Rose began his efforts to be reinstated so that he could manage in baseball and be voted into the Hall of Fame. He placed a petition on the Internet for fans to sign and appeared on various television shows. He appeared at Turner Field during the 1999 World Series as a member of the All-Century Team.

Hall of Fame Rule 21 states, "Voting shall be based upon the player's record, playing ability, integrity, sportsmanship, character, and contributions to the team(s) on which the player played." Yet players such as the unlikable Ty Cobb, the drinking and womanizing Babe Ruth, and the gambling Leo Durocher would not be in the Hall of Fame if their character were weighted over their talent.

➢ Should Pete Rose be reinstated?

➢ Should Pete Rose's baseball accomplishments be more important than his alleged betting on baseball?

Blood Transfusion

The Case of Colin and Rebecca

Colin and Rebecca were a happily married couple and parents of a thirteen-year-old son, John. All three family members were Jehovah's Witnesses. One day John complained about slight stomach pains, but his parents didn't worry about them because John often got nervous stomachaches. His pain, however, continued to worsen for about a week. On Monday, John went to school with stomach pain, and at noon Rebecca received a call that John had passed out after throwing up blood. He was rushed to the emergency room, and John was diagnosed with an ulcer. As a result of not going to the hospital sooner, he had lost a substantial amount of blood due to internal bleeding.

The doctors said that John's only chance to live was to receive a blood transfusion. This seemed like an easy situation, considering that doctors save the lives of people with ulcers daily, but Jehovah's Witnesses do not believe in blood transfusions, organ transplants, skin grafts, and vaccinations. The doctors urge the couple to let John receive the transfusion to avert their son's death.

➢ Should the hospital petition for a court order to impose the transfusion procedure?

➢ If the boy dies, should the parents be prosecuted for child neglect or endangerment?

The Case of the $10,000 Decision

Tom Johnson was the owner of a very successful machinery company outside of Boston. Johnson's Machinery was known for its fair treatment of customers and their good deals on machines. Tom took great pride in his reputation, but he still had to run a profitable business.

One day Patrick Gray came into the store to buy a machine from Johnson's Machinery. He sat down with one of the salesmen to work out a deal. Although Patrick was a frequent customer, he had a history of finding ways to get out of financial agreements. After an hour of debating, the salesman and Gray agreed on an amount of $150,000 for the machine that he was interested in purchasing. Johnson later came into the room to approve the agreement. When given the papers, Gray refused to sign them because his coworker was not there to approve. Instead, Johnson and Gray settled with a handshake until further notice.

An hour after Gray left, Stewart Shallow entered Johnson's Machinery. Shallow was one of Johnson's best and most valued customers. He had a history of fairness in his business deals with Johnson. Like Gray, Shallow sat down with a salesman and asked for the same machine in stock as Gray had. The problem arose when the salesman realized that this machine had already been claimed with a handshake. He informed Shallow of this problem. Shallow said that he must have the machine soon, and he could not wait for another one to come in. Johnson was then brought into the room with Shallow and the salesman. To further persuade Johnson, Shallow said he was ready to sign an agreement for $160,000 in exchange for the same machine.

Although legally Johnson had no ties with Gray, he still felt that he had some obligation to him. Gray also had a history of not being as good of a customer as Shallow. Shallow was one of Johnson's best customers, and Johnson wanted to please him so he would not buy this machine from another company.

➢ Should Johnson sell the machine to Gray or to Shallow?

➢ Could Johnson find another alternative?

The Case of Adam's Illness

Adam is a nineteen-year-old factory worker. When his father died of cancer two years ago, Adam dropped out of high school to help support his impoverished family. He is a model employee; he shows up for work on time, works very hard, and contributes to employee morale with his positive spirit.

Adam feels extremely sick at work one day. Afraid of the amount of the doctor's bill since he had not yet qualified for the company's health insurance policy, he postpones seeing a doctor. The unabated illness, however, finally prompts him to get an examination. The doctor's report is bad: he has cancer. Even worse, as a result of the delayed diagnosis, he only has an estimated two months to live.

Lisa Givens, the company's president, considers paying for Adam's doctor's bills even though he is not eligible for the company insurance policy. However, Keith, the company's business manager, expresses his concern that Lisa's generous act could set a dangerous precedent. He fears that other workers could expect and even sue the company for medical treatment not covered by the company's health program. Although he agrees that it would be good to help Adam in this crisis, he fears that bad consequences could ensue.

➢ Should the company look beyond the chance of being sued and help Adam?

➢ Could they find other ways to help him without risking legal and financial liability to others?

Church and State

High School Student Tackles Religion

David was beginning his senior year in high school. He had always been heavily involved in church. Growing up as a loyal Southern Baptist, David followed Jesus' teaching in Matthew to spread

His Word to everyone, which he did at school even though he did not impose his beliefs on others.

David had started two Christian-affiliated outreach programs that met once a week before school. He led by example on the basketball court and soccer field, which only added to the great respect his peers and teachers had for him. Even the non-Christian students and teachers respected him for his non-hypocritical lifestyle and his gracious spirit.

David's senior year began wonderfully. His clubs had high attendance, and many students were responding to the call of Christ in their lives; his life had never been more blessed. At the first football game, the whole school was excited because they were playing their big rivals at home. The game was closely contested; in the last quarter, their star player was running in for the touchdown that would pull their team ahead when two players tackled him simultaneously. A hush fell over the crowd as they waited for him to get up, but he would never rise again. He was paralyzed. The fans later learned that he had hurt himself in practice earlier that week but insisted on playing in the big game. Now he would never play or walk again.

The next week the halls were quiet and subdued. The incident had made the whole school aware of just how fast one's hopes and dreams, and even one's life, could be taken away. In order to bring the student body closer together again, David and his friends decided to have different students pray aloud before each football game. David and his friends thus submitted a proposal to the administration, but the administration regretfully explained to them that their proposal would violate the separation of church and state, and that they could only lead the audience in a moment of silence.

At the next football game, David planned to lead the audience in a moment of silence; however, he felt led by God's Spirit to pray aloud. He went to the loudspeaker and asked everyone to bow his or her head and pray with him. He then prayed a prayer that moved the hearts of most fans. Unfortunately, school officials were not so pleased. Although they too were touched by David's prayer, the school rules dictated that David should be suspended or even expelled.

In the following weeks the administration held several meetings with David and his parents, and David repeatedly told them that he would do it again if given the chance. Students and adults from surrounding cities wrote letters on David's behalf, and other students also began to lead prayers instead of a moment of silence. The administration was stuck between a rock and a hard place. If they expelled David, he would become a martyr; if they suspended him, they would become the villains; and if they did nothing, it could be said that they bent the rules for the "good" kids.

➢ Was David's action justifiable?

➢ Should the administration make an example of David even though he was an exemplary student and person?

➢ Should the other students continue to defy what they consider to be an unjust rule?

Divorce

The Case of Bob's Divorce

Bob, who lived in Seattle, was a very respected doctor. He had everything going for him: an undergraduate degree from Duke, a medical degree from Vanderbilt, a loving wife, Carol, two loving daughters, Ashley and Caroline, and ample money. Bob, notwithstanding external appearances, felt a deep sense of malaise.

Since he was the team doctor for an arena football team in Seattle, he traveled with the team to a game in St. Louis. While at a bar, Bob met a woman named Laura who was about five years younger than he. Believing that his relationship with Carol was unsatisfying, Bob kept in touch with Laura via e-mail, and Laura soon became one of the most important people in the world to Bob. She could assuage his angst and meet his emotional and sexual needs.

Bob decided that Laura was his soul mate. He shocked Carol by informing her he wanted a divorce because he was in love with another woman. Bob convinced Carol not to tell their daughters about the divorce until he "found the right time."

One day Ashley, who was fourteen, decided to get online for a school project. She inadvertently found a love letter from Laura to her father. She was outraged by the discovery of this letter, and after confronting her father, further angered by her parents keeping their marital failure a secret from her and Caroline.

Laura then moved to Seattle, presumably to marry Bob after his divorce, and Bob wanted his daughters to meet and welcome Laura into their lives. Caroline, who was eleven, accepted Laura to protect her relationship with her father. Ashley refused to let this woman into her life, and likewise wanted to have nothing to do with her father. Her school grades fell, and she began to act out sexually with boys.

Although Carol was initially disturbed by Bob's affair and disregard for his marriage and family, she later found another man who made her happier than Bob ever did. Caroline loved Laura as her own mother, and even Ashley eventually adjusted to the new family arrangements.

➢ Did Bob's and everyone else's eventual happiness justify his divorce?

The Minister's Decision

Linda Franklin is a thirty-four year old waitress. She has been married to Tom for about nine years. They have two children: Cindy, who is six, and Jonathan, who is eight. The family faithfully attends church, except for Tom.

One day Linda calls the pastor's office and asks to see him. At their appointment, she expresses concern for her marriage and for the welfare of the children. She tells the pastor that her husband has recently lost his job as a construction worker due to his regular failure to show up at work. Linda is now trying to support her two children, her husband, and herself, but Tom spends money every night on beer, which greatly upsets Linda. Sometimes after Tom has been drinking, he verbally abuses her and the kids.

Before he lost his job, and especially when he was not drinking, Tom was generally pleasant and attentive to the children. Linda tells the minister that she is afraid that he does not want to get a job and that his current demeanor is not good for the children. Besides offering her support and comfort, the pastor recommends marital counseling for her and Tom.

A month later, while Tom is still jobless, Linda tells the pastor that Tom resists counseling and that his drinking and temper are getting worse. The minister offers to do individual crisis counseling to help Linda cope with the situation. They agree to meet again because Linda is extremely worried about her children.

After several more weeks, Linda again meets with the pastor and begins to realize that Tom's behavior is unacceptable and that her love and concern for the children are greater than that for her husband. After this session, the pastor realizes that he and Linda are in a difficult situation. On one hand, Linda says she no longer loves Tom and is concerned for her children's well-being, but on the other hand, while Tom's behavior is unacceptable, he and Linda took Christian vows of marriage "for better or worse, till death do us part." The minister believes that the Bible speaks strongly against the practice of divorce, but he also observes that the children are suffering and potentially endangered because of their father's disposition. Linda has decided to move out of the house and to seek a legal separation while she considers divorce. She has asked the minister to support her course of action.

➢ What should the minister do?

Drug Abuse

The Case of Charles and Suzie

Charles Smith, a well-respected doctor, lives in a small town with his wife and four children. An honest, generous family, they try to lead the best Christian lifestyle they can. The community respects Charles as much for his impeccable character and good decision-making ability as for his excellent medical skills.

Over the past few weeks, a few pre-med students have been running errands, watching doctors work, and scrubbing in on surgeries. One capable intern, Suzie, shows great promise as a physician. Dr. Smith has great confidence in her and is impressed with her diligence and compassion. She demonstrates a deep concern for patients and performs her tasks with precision.

One night Dr. Smith receives a phone call from a local pharmacy wanting to know whether or not he had filled out a prescription for 30 mg of Percocet, a narcotic otherwise known as Oxycodone, for Suzie. Dr. Smith does not remember doing so, but since he cannot be positive, he asks the pharmacy to fax him a copy of the prescription. Upon receiving the copy, Dr. Smith knows his signature had been forged. He informs the pharmacy that it is not his signature, and they ask him if he wants to press charges. He knows if he presses charges against Suzie, her medical career would be ruined. She would go to jail and would never be able to become the doctor she is capable of becoming. He knows, however, that Suzie committed a crime, and if he does not turn her in, she could do it again. He wants to give her a second chance, but he also wants to consider the lives of others who could be potentially endangered if he does not press charges.

> Should Dr. Smith overlook Suzie's crime or should he report her to the authorities?

The Case of Samantha

The Romans had just moved to a new suburb in Dallas from their old home in Ohio. Their daughter, Samantha, who recently turned sixteen, started attending the local high school, Greendale. Samantha was very upset at the move because she had to leave behind all her very close friends whom she had known since preschool. She was very angry at her parents. She had never been a defiant child, but since the move she voiced a rude comment about anything and everything that her parents asked her to do. She often left her mother in tears after an argument.

After two months in school, Samantha's parents began to notice that she had not made any new friends. She came home day after day, weekend after weekend, and watched television. She never received any phone calls or went out with friends. The most peculiar thing was that Samantha never went out on any dates even though she was a pretty girl and had been very popular back in Ohio. The very next weekend, however, Samantha asked her mother if she could have a party at their house. Her parents jumped at the chance to throw a party for their recently withdrawn daughter.

The big night arrived after what seemed like endless hours of cleaning house and buying and preparing food. Around 8:00 dozens of teenagers started to arrive at the Romans' ranch, and luckily they had ordered enough pizza to satisfy all the guests. After about an hour, Samantha's parents decided to move the party into the old barn where the music blared and Samantha gleamed. The Romans decided to go to bed around midnight and trusted Samantha to be responsible. After all, she had always been a very trustworthy, obedient girl, and only about fifteen guests remained at the party.

After Samantha's parents went to bed, Kent, one of Samantha's guests, opened a huge bottle of vodka. He poured it into the bowl of punch as the other guests cheered. They all began to drink the punch, and an hour later they were all very drunk. Five of the boys piled into Kent's Explorer and proceeded to go home. Samantha, who was less drunk than the rest, tried to stop them, only to be left in their dust. She then went back into the barn and went to sleep on a cot amongst the other guests, who had already passed out.

In the morning Samantha was awakened by the shrill of her parents' screaming. She learned that the boys who had left in Kent's Explorer had been in a terrible accident. Two of the boys were in the intensive care unit with head wounds, and another boy broke his neck after he flew out of the car when it hit a tree head-on. The other two boys, including Kent and his designated driver, who drank the least of all the boys, escaped with only cuts and bruises. The police investigation uncovered that Kent's parents had given him the vodka to take to the party and that Samantha's parents went to sleep while the teenage party kept going past midnight in their barn.

- Should Kent, who was underage, be held legally responsible for bringing vodka to the party?

- Should Kent's parents, who provided vodka for the party, be the ones to blame for the wreck?

- Should the designated driver bear liability for the damage to the Explorer?

- Should the Romans be punished for being negligent chaperones even though they didn't supply the boys with the vodka?

The Case of Scott

Judge Scott Jonathan Richard III is a seventy-three-year-old gentleman. He and his wife, Anne, have two children and six grandchildren. Both of their children, Lisa and Patrick, live within five miles of them. Scott and Anne have been happily married for forty-eight years and have lived through many ups and downs together. Scott has always supported his family in all their decisions. He supported Lisa in her quest to be a doctor, Patrick in his quest to become a Methodist minister, and Anne when she went back to school to be a nurse practitioner. Life was going well for Scott and his family.

One morning things began to change. While at his eldest grandson's championship tee-ball game, Scott complained of a sudden numbness in his leg. Anne proposed that they should leave the game and go to the hospital, but Scott did not want to miss any of the game, saying that his leg probably just fell asleep. Anne was not happy with his decision but could not persuade Scott to leave.

As the officials were handing out trophies to his grandson's team, Scott's arm became numb. Anne rushed him to the hospital. Soon after they arrived, the doctors informed the couple that Scott had been experiencing warning signs of a stroke. Despite medical treatment, Scott had an extensive stroke and slipped into a coma. His children were called and immediately went to the hospital. They waited all night, but Scott still showed no sign of waking up from the coma. The next day, the doctor walked in and told the family that there was only a small chance that Scott could regain consciousness. He further explained that if Scott did wake up, he would probably be paralyzed.

The family must now decide whether or not Scott should be taken off of life support. Lisa underscores the bleak medical prognosis, but Patrick opposes taking him off life support irrespective of his prognosis. Anne is torn between Patrick and Lisa and is unsure of what she wants to do. Scott's life is in her hands.

➤ Should Anne listen to Patrick or to Lisa?

➤ Is the chance of letting Scott remain in a coma or live with disabilities more ethical than letting him die a peaceful death?

Homosexuality

The Case of One Fewer Couple

Unlike many workplaces in the United States, the employers of *Smart and Simple* magazine encouraged its employees to date their coworkers. They thought that this would make the workplace more enjoyable and friendly. When Blake joined the team of over fifty others at the magazine as a fashion editor, this idea appealed to him greatly. Since Blake was gay, he already felt uncomfortable at most other workplaces. When he signed on at *Smart and Simple,* he was pleased to find out that there were about ten other gay employees. His first week went well as he made friends and started to become comfortable around others. He noticed many straight couples flirting throughout the day and discovered that two couples in the business were married.

Over the next few months, he started going out with his buddies after work for drinks and became interested in Leo. He was funny, smart, cute, and in Blake's opinion, all that he had ever wanted in a man. Meanwhile, at work, Blake was moving up. He had just received an award as September's best editor out of hundreds of other magazines and over many co-workers. His co-workers expressed how excited they were for him and told him that he definitely deserved this award. Blake was truly surprised by how open, warm, and accepting they were of him. He had never been around people who had treated him so respectfully. Usually when people discovered that he was gay, they acted rudely towards him.

A few months later, Blake and Leo announced that they were going to live together and form a permanent partnership. His coworkers seemed a bit surprised yet happy for the both of them. After all, this wasn't the first time that two people at *Smart and Simple* magazine lived together or became "married." Like the other couples, Blake and Leo flirted mildly but did not engage in what one would call "heavy flirting." They tried to keep a professional relationship while at the office.

On Blake's thirtieth birthday, he and Leo were called into their employer's office. Rochelle, their boss, told both men that their relationship was causing discomfort among their co-workers. She told them that their co-workers had complained that their flirting was distracting and unprofessional. She said that she agreed with the workers, which left Blake and Leo dumbfounded. She gave them a week to improve their behavior. They refused and asked why the other married and dating couples who flirted were not being reprimanded. She explained that no one had complained about them. She restated her offer that they could have a week to improve their behavior. Blake and Leo both flatly refused her offer. They said they were being discriminated against because they were gay. Leo said that they were acting the way most couples act.

Their fellow gay workers stood strongly behind Blake and Leo and wrote a letter of protest. They pointed out that straight couples at *Smart and Simple* flirted just as much as Blake and Leo. Blake had been an exceptional employee and editor for the magazine, and he did not deserve to lose his job. Rochelle ignored the letter, so Blake and Leo brought a lawsuit against *Smart and Simple* for discrimination against gays.

➤ Is Rochelle right in asking Blake and Leo to "clean up" their act? Or is she guilty of discriminating against gays?

The Case of Tommy and Bryan

Tommy and Bryan are both in their late twenties. They have been in a stable, monogamous relationship since college. During college they both worked at a local day care center for underprivileged children where they established wonderful relationships with the children. Tommy graduated with a bachelor's degree in accounting and is now a successful banker. Bryan graduated with a bachelor's degree in computer technology and is now working on his master's degree. He owns an internet company and therefore has flexible hours.

Both attend church and are God-fearing men, and they would like to adopt children. Tommy is a deacon at their church, and Bryan teaches Sunday school to preschoolers. Tommy comes from a large family and has four siblings and many nieces and nephews. His parents have been happily married for forty-two years. Bryan's parents were married for fifteen years but then divorced. His father is involved in a homosexual relationship, but Bryan had already realized his sexual orientation at this point. Bryan's two brothers are both happily married with families of their own. Tommy and Bryan would provide a loving environment for children to develop. They are financially stable, able to spend time with the children, and have experience with young children. They committed themselves through a marriage ceremony, although not a legally binding one, and believe that they have the ability to raise children as well as any heterosexual couple.

➤ Should Tommy and Bryan be able to legally marry?

157

➤ Should homosexuals be allowed to adopt children?

Honor

The Case of Kevin and Todd

Todd Janssen and Kevin Wallace have been best friends for as long as they can remember. They are both in the eleventh grade at a small private school in New Jersey, and both are regarded by their school's faculty as being honorable, courteous, and respectful of others. Neither has ever gotten into any serious trouble. In fact, the faculty recently recommended Todd to be a member of the highly esteemed student honor committee. However, Kevin has witnessed several incidents in the past when Todd cheated on tests, "borrowed" other students' books without asking, or lied to friends, and the school's honor code explicitly states that no student shall lie, cheat, or steal. Kevin has confronted Todd about his actions, but Todd claims that he has not done anything that is wrong.

Kevin does not feel that Todd is qualified for a place on the honor committee, but he resists telling the faculty. Later, students vote for whomever they believe would best exemplify the principles of the school. Todd, being a popular student and clever at concealing his moral misdeeds, receives the most votes for his class and is appointed a position on the honor committee. Kevin struggles with the decision of whether or not to tell the faculty the truth of his companion's past.

The situation worsens when Kevin discovers that his friend still cheats on tests and lies to teachers on a regular basis. Todd even cheats and lies more frequently at this point, taking advantage of his position on the honor committee by knowing that no one would accuse him of committing an honor offense. No one would even consider that Todd is dishonest.

Kevin knows that what Todd is doing is morally wrong, but he is too afraid to tell anyone the truth for fear that no one will believe him. Kevin's main concern is for the fairness of the frequent decisions that the honor committee makes regarding fellow peers' alleged honor offenses. Kevin would also jeopardize his lifelong friendship with Todd, however, if he reported him as an honor offender.

➤ Should Kevin confront Todd again and tell him that if he continues to violate the honor code, Kevin will tell the rest of the committee members?

➤ What if Kevin did nothing, and just let the matter sort itself out? Is someone bound to find out about Todd's secret misdeeds anyway?

➤ Would it be fair to the rest of the students at school and the honor policy if Kevin said nothing?

➤ What should Kevin do?

The Case of Jesse and Jack

Jesse and Jack Matthews are identical twins who grew up in a traditional family in Blount County, Tennessee. Their family was very close-knit, and they learned good morals and values. Whenever anyone had a problem or uncomfortable situation, the whole family would discuss it and pray about it.

Jesse and Jack remained very close throughout middle and high school. They were both on the football and soccer teams in middle school, and they took the same classes in high school. When they started dating, they would often go out on double dates with their girlfriends; sometimes they would switch places as a joke on their girlfriends. The relationship between Jesse and Jack also remained close during their first year of college at the University of Tennessee when Jesse began drinking heavily.

During his first year in college, Jesse met a girl named Amanda. By his fourth year there, they were married and had a baby boy. Jesse's drinking habits slowed down when his son Mark was born, but by the time Mark was two, Jesse drank more than ever. When Mark was three, Amanda decided that she had had enough of Jesse's alcoholism, so she divorced him and moved out with Mark. The divorce depressed Jesse, and he plunged deeper into alcohol abuse.

When Jack graduated from the University of Tennessee, he got married, went to medical school at Vanderbilt, and became a doctor. By the time Amanda had divorced Jesse, Jack had two children

160

and another was on the way. When Amanda spoke with Jack about Jesse's drinking problem, Jack brought it to the attention of the entire family and suggested that Jesse go to a rehabilitation center to get his life back on track. Jesse knew that he had a problem, so he willingly went to the rehabilitation center and began a recovery.

Jesse was released from rehab several months later and no longer drinks. About three years have passed since he finished rehab, but now Jesse has an even larger problem. The drinking ravaged his liver, and he needs a transplant as soon as possible. Jesse has been put onto a donor list, but given his rare blood type, he would probably die while waiting. Jack is a perfect match and could be a partial liver donor without incurring a significant morbidity risk.

➤ Should Jack undergo this procedure even though Jesse's behavior caused the problem or insist that Jack take his chances with the waiting list?

School Violence

School Tensions at Lincoln High

Jeffrey is a tenth grader at Lincoln High School in Sacramento, California. An average student, he struggles to find his place at school. Because he is poorer than the majority of his peers, he faces daily ridicule for his ragged attire.

Jeffrey begs his parents to move and tells them how the other kids treat him, but since his family does not have much money, they cannot afford to move. He and his parents are Christians, and his parents tell him that since he has Jesus in his heart, nothing else should matter.

Jeffrey does not find solace in their counsel. He and his less affluent friends begin wearing long coats and dressing in black. They become known as the "Rebels" and threaten to kill anyone that makes fun of them. Jeffrey's parents become worried and try to get him to go to church, but he angrily refuses. He and his friends decide that the only way to get any respect from their peers would be to do something drastic. They plan to go into school one day with guns to find everyone that had ever made fun of them and kill them. Jeffrey also plans to kill everyone that is a Christian because he is angry with God for putting him in a situation where he is known as "that poor kid." The following day, the Rebels gun down many students and several teachers before killing themselves.

➢ What could have mitigated these tensions (consider currently proposed measures such as gun control laws and dress codes)?

Sex

The Case of Cajun Nights

John DeWalt was the sole owner of a small
Cajun restaurant named Dante's Kitchen in Atlanta,
Georgia. He was working on the books at his
restaurant one evening when a young woman
complained about her meal. After discussing it with
his cook and determining the waiter was in error,
John had the cook prepare the dish correctly and
then delivered it himself.

The woman he took the meal to was stunning.
She wore a tasteful black dress with a pearl necklace,
and she was dining alone. Surprisingly, when he
delivered the meal, she requested that he sit and
join her. Tired of calculating numbers and lured by
her beauty, he decided to join her. Many glasses of
wine and an hour or so later, he told the chef to lock
up while John accompanied this sumptuous woman
back to her place.

After spending the night together, John
returned home the next morning feeling younger than
he had since his wife had passed away about four
years earlier. He was now fifty-three years old, and a
night with this beautiful woman in her mid-twenties
revitalized him. He did not see her for a few months
until she came in again and asked to speak to the
owner. The situation repeated itself. After that
night, she disappeared from his life for another three
months until one evening when he convinced his
twenty-six-year old daughter to bring a few of her
friends to try the restaurant so that its name could
circulate. As his daughter walked in, he realized with

163

abject horror that Sue, one of his daughter's best friends, was really Susan, the woman with whom he had spent nights of passion. The meal passed without incident. John stopped by the table briefly, but thankfully Susan said nothing about their relationship.

Since then, he and Susan have talked about their relationship but could not decide if they should tell Joan, his daughter, about it. Susan felt that he should not tell Joan so that they could continue the relationship in secret. Since John's wife died, however, he has never really held anything back from his daughter and still felt awful about not having told her about his relationship with her friend.

➢ Should John tell Joan and discontinue the relationship, tell Joan and still continue the relationship, continue the relationship in secret, or discontinue the relationship and not tell Joan?

Sex Education

The Case of Kari

Kari Ray's eighth grade public school guidance class deals with lifestyle issues, including premarital sex, sexually transmitted diseases, and pregnancy. Kari and her boyfriend Mitch have sex, even though they know that abstinence is the only 100% effective way to avoid sexually transmitted diseases (STDs) or pregnancy, but they do practice "safe sex," as she learned in her guidance class, by using condoms.

164

Despite their precautions, Kari is now pregnant. Her mother Nancy has just found out and is devastated. Nancy believes that even though Kari should have known better, the school is partly at fault for not emphasizing abstinence as the only way to be safe from STDs or pregnancy.

The following week, John Waters, the Director of the Board of Education for Union County, Tennessee, plans to hold a public meeting for parents of schoolchildren to discuss an "abstinence-only" sex education program. All parents are informed of the meeting through the mail and are urged to attend. If the Union County schools are going to start this new program this year, they have to decide in two weeks so that the materials can be shipped and the teachers trained. Nancy Ray was one of the many who chose to attend the meeting.

On the day of the meeting, Kari also finds out that she had acquired herpes from her boyfriend. He had lied to her about being a virgin and also concealed having a sexually transmitted disease. Nancy is furious when she leaves for the city-county building and still shocked that something like this could happen to her daughter.

The meeting opens with a brief message from Mr. Waters, who says, "Our children are our country's greatest asset. They are the rising leaders and lawmakers, and they are our country's greatest hope for a better society and world, but some of them are being shortchanged. Their opportunities and dreams are being flushed down the drain because they are making bad decisions—choosing to have sex before they are married and suffering the harsh and sometimes fatal consequences of their decisions.

165

Besides the physical effects of premarital sex, harmful psychological effects can occur. Our precious children feel regret, guilt, and shame; they feel betrayed and used, and they worry about their future. No one should feel this way. Our loved ones need to be educated; they need to be told the truth, and they need to be taught in the best way possible."

When he finishes, everyone in the building is silent. Finally, the secretary for the Board of Education rises and announces the next speaker, a doctor from the Health Department in Memphis. Dr. Sharon Malley is going to provide everyone with information about pregnancy rates. She reports, "Less than one third of the teens who begin a family before age eighteen ever complete high school. Although adolescent pregnancy rates are decreasing in Tennessee, they remain high." After marshalling ample statistical evidence to support her point, the crowd is astonished that so many girls in the state and in their own county are getting pregnant.

The next speaker, Dr. Brady, is also from the Department of Health, and he has information about the new abstinence-only education program. "This program," he emphasizes, "teaches the positive aspects of abstaining from sexual activity. It teaches that sex outside of marriage is unacceptable. It promotes abstinence as the only sure way to avoid STDs."

For discussion, parents are instructed to raise their hand, ask a question, or make a comment when the microphone is passed to them, and then wait for a response. Nancy Ray is the first person to raise her hand. She receives the microphone, rises, and asks, "What have you been teaching our children up

166

until now?" Mr. Prock explains that the children are currently taught that abstinence is the only 100% way to be safe, but they are also taught about contraceptives in case they did decide to have sex.

Another woman in the crowd raises her hand to ask, "If we choose not to tell our children about birth control and other contraceptives, are we not lying to them? I mean, yes, abstinence is the only certain way to prevent pregnancy, but birth control and condoms usually do work. So if we tell them that abstinence is the only way, it's as if we're lying." A man angrily retorts, "I teach my daughter to wait until marriage, and I don't want anyone teaching her to use contraceptives."

Vigorous discussion ensues for about forty-five minutes, and Mr. Waters encourages parents to talk to their children about sex and abstinence. He also informs them that the Board of Education must decide whether or not to endorse the new abstinence-only program.

➢ What should the Board of Education do, and why?

➢ Who should assume the responsibility to educate children about sex, and why?

Sexual Abuse

The Case of Jenny

Jenny Roberts is a seven-year-old girl who has two older brothers, Brian and Michael. The Roberts are very active in their church and community. Practically all of their relatives live in the same small town that they do. Jenny's uncle, Big Mike, owns a successful law firm and is very respected by everyone in the town except Jenny. Big Mike has been secretly sexually abusing Jenny since she was about four years old. Jenny is very ashamed and extremely afraid of what Big Mike will do if she tells on him.

As Jenny gets older, the abuse worsens. When Jenny is ready to enter high school, she begs her parents to send her away to a boarding school instead of following in her older brothers' and cousins' footsteps by going to the local high school. Her parents finally agree to let her go since the school is only a few hours away, and Jenny is very excited that she will be escaping Big Mike's abuse.

Jenny graduates from the boarding school having visited home as little as possible over the past four years. On these rare visits, however, Big Mike does manage to continue his abuse. Jenny is now in great need of psychological counseling; when she goes to college, she finally breaks down. She starts seeing a counselor twice a week without the knowledge of any of her family members. After two years of therapy, she feels that she can finally move on from her past.

During this time, Jenny meets a great guy, David. David and Jenny fall in love. After they both complete college, they decide to get married. David looks for work for many months without success. While talking to her mother on the phone, Jenny gets the idea that David could work in Big Mike's firm. Brian, Michael, and many of Jenny's cousins already work at the firm, and it would be a great job for

David. Also, Jenny has recently found out that she and David will be having their first child, so she is excited at the prospect of moving back to her home town.

Everything goes as planned while Jenny and David get settled into their new life, and Jenny feels ready to forgive Big Mike. Big Mike has been going to counseling for many years now. He feels extremely sorry for abusing Jenny as a child, and he also feels that he is completely over his problem.

Jenny and David have a baby girl, Bethany, and for the next five years, life seems perfect. Family get-togethers are the only times that Bethany is really exposed to Big Mike, and in her five years of life she has never been alone with him. One day, however, Big Mike calls Jenny to see if Bethany can come to a baseball game with him. He says that he only has two tickets and really wants to spend some quality time with Bethany. Jenny believes that Big Mike is a changed man, and she values David's employment in Big Mike's company, but she still fears what could happen.

➤ Should Jenny allow Bethany to go to the baseball game?